ESSAY on MIND

ESSAY on MIND

D. O. Hebb

Dalhousie University

LEA LAWRENCE ERLBAUM ASSOCIATES, PUBLISHERS
1980   Hillsdale, New Jersey

Lawrence Erlbaum Associates, Inc., Publishers
365 Broadway
Hillsdale, New Jersey 07642

Library of Congress Cataloging in Publication Data

Hebb, Donald Olding.
  Essay on mind.

  Bibliography: p.
  Includes indexes.
  1. Psychology—Philosophy.   2. Neuropsychology.
I. Title.
BF38.H43   153   79-24993
ISBN 0-89859-017-5

Printed in the United States of America

Contents

Preface

My hope with this book is to contribute to the understanding of mind and thought. I attempt this as one whose psychological research has been behavioristic and biological in its orientation, concerned with the functions of the nervous system and with such things as the evolution of mental processes or the effect of the early environment—but also as one who has been concerned about the nature of mind or the meaning of consciousness, and the question of lawfulness in the universe and in human behavior. The result is that this book may seem to be a mixture of unrelated topics, partly psychology, partly philosophy.

But the topics are not unrelated, and the book has its own kind of unity. Einstein considered that philosophy is essential for the scientist, a living influence on scientific thought. If that is true in physics it must be at least as true in psychology. The object of my work has been to learn about thought, the central problem of psychology—but also, not less important, to learn how to think clearly about thought, which is philosophy. I have not found the task easy. Modern psychology is professedly objective and scientific, which is its strength, but old habits of thought persist unrecognized. I have dealt with them—to the extent that I *have* dealt with them—only by trying to make explicit my ideas about the nature of mind, about self-knowledge, about determinism and freedom of thought ("free will"). These are topics that may affect psychological research whether the researcher recognizes it or not. Then there is also the effect of the physical-science model of the scientific method. Should we, for example, be trying to establish psychological laws in a way that would parallel the great physical laws?

But I have also found suggestions of a converse effect on philosophy from unrecognized behavioral ideas. Any form of monism or dualism tacitly implies a theory of behavior. Descartes made his theory of behavior explicit, but subsequent generations of philosophers did not. The result is that some modern philosophic views are still influenced by primitive 17th-century conceptions of the nervous system. In the text I have tried to show that there is a logical flaw in philosophic idealism that becomes apparent when the behavioral implications are made explicit. Psychology and philosophy were divorced some time ago, but like other divorced couples they still have problems in common.

Thus I hope to interest both psychologist and philosopher. The level of difficulty is meant to be suitable for the graduate student and the senior undergraduate—and I hope, for the interested layman.

The first three chapters are methodological and philosophic; preparation and perhaps justification for the biologically oriented theory of behavior that is developed in Chapters 4 to 8. These five chapters deal with the evolution of mind, the still-confused nature-nurture question, how the cell-assembly idea originated, the infant's development of thought and language regarded as primarily perceptual learning, and the cell-assembly idea brought up to date in applying it to the understanding of creative thought and Hilgard's recent surprising results with hypnosis.

Chapters 9 and 10 turn finally to the way in which the thought of the physical scientist works in practice (not how the books say it works). This is not because I think scientific thought is all that different from other thought, but because of the available record of practical problem-solving over a period of centuries. The conclusions arrived at seem to fit the thought of laymen as well, and they contain some surprises. For example, it appears that determinism is a logical necessity, not something about which one has a choice. I am more than surprised at having reached such a conclusion, and I will be interested to see the refutation. Finally, it appears in Chapter 10 that a scientist, like other human beings, lives and works in a world of the imagination, never being able to know directly the things he or she is most concerned with, a fact that must be taken into account when considering the meaning of scientific law. Human beings are a thought-dominated species.

The scope of the book is limited, restricted mostly to topics on which it seemed to me that I had a present contribution to make. There is no pretence at a scholarly review of the literature, as the reader will see by looking at my references. These are however ones that are still relevant to fundamental questions.

I am indebted for ideas and valuable criticism to more colleagues and former graduate students than I can mention here. On several occasions an old friend, George A. Miller, has saved me from embarrassing revelations of ignorance. Over a period of years I have had similar help and support from

Dalbir Bindra, Peter Milner, Ronald Melzack, and the late Sam Rabinovitch. It is a pleasure to record my indebtedness. It is also a pleasure to acknowledge the competent skill of a series of secretaries, over the same long period, and particularly Jane Corcoran, Celia Jeffreys, and Audrey Bennett.

Preparation of the final manuscript was assisted by the award of an Isaak Walton Killam Scholarship from the Canada Council, for which I am indeed grateful.

D. O. Hebb

ESSAY on MIND

1 Mind as a Biological Problem

This book seeks an increased understanding of the human mind from a biological approach that affects some long-standing philosophic problems as well as psychological ones. Mind is the central psychological problem, although it is no longer fashionable to say so; psychologists prefer to talk about "cognitive processes" instead. They also prefer, most of them, to abstain from discussion of what those processes consist of and how their effects are achieved. But unless one is a dualist one must agree that it is the brain that thinks, and what I try to show here is that it is of interest and even enlightening to ask how the brain does the trick.

This book proposes that such neurologizing adds significantly to our understanding; that mind and thought, consciousness and creativity and free will, are all biologically evident phenomena and seen most clearly in the light of evolutionary ideas; and that looking at human beings as higher animals and mental activity as an activity of the brain does not degrade man but on the contrary enhances one's respect for that species.

Some of the discussion concerns a specific theory of brain function (that cell-assemblies are the basis of thought) and its meaning for certain classical problems, but we will also be concerned more broadly with aspects of human thought to which the theory makes no specific contribution. However, the behavioral point of view itself, apart from any theory, affects one's perception of the fundamentals of scientific thought and even of the logic of dualism, or of determinism. It is inaccurate—worse, it is misleading—to call psychology the study of behavior: It is the study of the underlying processes, just as chemistry is the study of the atom rather than pH values, spectroscopes, and test tubes; but behavior *is* the primary source of data in modern psychology and looking from that objective point of view at the ideas of philosophic idealism, or the problem of the self and self-knowledge, or the place of law and determinism in scientific thought, lets one see things that as far as I can make out have not been seen before. These are philosophic questions but they are fundamental for psychology too, if psychology is to be a science and avoid the Scylla and Charybdis of outright positivism on the one hand and literary fantasy on the other. All science, from physics to physiology, is a function of its philosophic presuppositions, but psychology is more vulnerable than others to the effect of misconception in fundamental matters because the object of its study is after all the human mind and the nature of human thought, and it is very easy for philosophic ideas about the soul, for example, or about determinism and free will, to affect the main lines of theory. As long as the ideas are implicit they are dangerous; make them explicit and perhaps they can be defused.

In proposing that psychology is the study of the mind, but from a more or less biological stance, I do not for a moment suggest that students of perception, or memory, or language, or motivation and emotion, should change their research interests. On the contrary: These are all avenues to an increased understanding of the processes that control behavior, and *that* is our common objective. I certainly do not propose that all psychologists should be doing comparative animal studies or operating on the brain, or even that the black-box approach to behavior—refusal to take account of the brain in theorizing—should be ruled out, although that approach cannot be the most productive line in the long run. Tolman and Hull in the 30's and 40's were both black-box men, for example, as most cognitive psychologists are today; and ethology, which is by definition the biological study of behavior, has never concerned itself greatly with the brain.

The point is rather that the central body of psychological thought is much closer to ethology, physiology and genetics than to economics or even to sociology. Looked at as one of the social sciences, psychology is conspicuous as the only one that is experimental (one might say narrowly experimental, obsessively concerned with questions of method) and the only one that aims at the study of mechanisms in the individual subject. There is a well-developed specialty called social psychology, which certainly sounds like social science; but social behavior can be considered from a biological point of view. Also, since about 1950, social psychology has become primarily experimental and it has always dealt with the individual in social situations. This is shown by the traditionally close relation of social psychology to personality study, and more recently by "attribution theory" (which is concerned with the determinants of response in social situations). The concern of sociology is with social structures and organizations; that of social psychology with the causes of individual behavior in this or that social situation.

Before going on I must make sure that the reader understands how I use such terms as mind and consciousness. The word *mind* for some psychologists necessarily implies mysticism, but that is wrong. Broadly speaking, the mind is that which controls behavior (the larger aspects of man's behavior, that is, excluding the purely reflexive and not worrying at this point about the question of mind in other higher animals). And broadly speaking, there are two ideas about this something that controls: one that it is spiritual or immaterial, the other that it is a physical activity of the brain. The idea that mind is a spirit is a theory of demonic possession, a form of the vitalism that biology got rid of a century ago. It means that a waking, thinking, conscious human being is conscious because his body is inhabited by a spirit (or daemon, which is how "demon" can be spelled to show that it is maybe a good demon). This is *dualism,* the idea that there are two totally different kinds of existence, mind and matter, and it is—for the present at least—a stumbling-block for the scientific approach to understanding man. As we will see, it cannot be disproved, which means that it may possibly be right; but the scientific procedure nevertheless, in the present state of our knowledge, must be to assume that it is wrong and see how far we can get on that basis.

The alternative is *monism,* the idea that mind and matter are not fundamentally different but different forms of the same thing: in practice in psychology, the idea that mental processes are brain processes. The idea is held tacitly more often than not, but it has been the scientifically productive one in the psychology of this century, and the present essay is an attempt to take that line a step further.

My general position can be put precisely: Mind is the capacity for thought (thus one still has a mind when one is unconscious on the operating table, or in deep sleep): consciousness, a variable state, is a present activity of thought processes in some form; and thought itself is an activity of the brain. I may anticipate the later discussion to the extent of saying that thought is not any brain activity, but one that can occur in the absence of the thing thought about, as for example in the memory image. Another example is invention, when one thinks of something that has not been seen or heard of before. Most thought is directly related to or excited by what is now present, but it is not limited to the present situation, and it always tends to be creative in some degree.

What about the computer? Does it think, and if so does that make it conscious? For the present at least, the answer is that it does not think in the sense that human beings and other mammals think and so is not conscious in the same sense. Furthermore, the mammalian brain is enormously more complex than any present computer, not only in the number of functional elements but also in its connections, the individual neuron frequently having synaptic connection with upwards of a thousand others. What I propose is that we have here a parallel with the physicist's concept of a critical mass. Consciousness, that is, depends on a critical degree of complexity of neural action. Probably also it requires the kind or pattern of complexity characteristic of the structure of mammalian cortex. The individual neuron then is not conscious, nor any small group of interacting neurons. Consciousness appeared in evolution when thought became possible, and there is no evidence of thought in lower animals, even those with quite extensive nervous systems. It probably exists in birds such as the crow, but it has not actually been demonstrated except in mammals. In them the cortex is well developed, but vestigial or absent in other animal forms.

The argument then is that a computer built on the plan of the mammalian brain, and of a complexity at least equal to that of the brain of the laboratory rat, might be conscious—given the same capacity to learn and a suitable early experience. This is unlikely, but conceivable.

THE OBJECTIONS TO IDENTITY THEORY

The theory that there is an identity of mind with some activity of the brain may be rejected on the basis simply of common sense, or it may be rejected because of one or other of various disproofs that—apparently—show that the theory is impossible. We will come back, later in this chapter, to the question of how far common sense can be trusted as a criticism of a scientific theory— not very far, it seems, since common sense is a peculiar combination of wisdom and error, fact and fantasy, and science in other fields than psychology is full of ideas that to common sense would seem like nonsense if it were not that they turn out to be true, no matter how peculiar they may have looked at first. That point will be returned to. Here let us consider some of the attempts to give a specific disproof of identity theory.

The trouble with most of these attempts is that they take for granted something that appears not to be true: that there is immediate knowledge of one's own mental processes. We will see in the following chapter what reason there is to doubt that this is so. The critic, however, talks as if one need only consider one's own thoughts in order to see that thought or perception or emotion is not what identity theory implies. What the criticism really does is mistake older theoretical ideas for observed fact. We do of course know something of what goes on in our own minds but—as we will see—the knowledge depends on inference. I look out of the window and perceive a tree, but I do not perceive the perception, to know how perception occurs; I imagine a monster and know what the imagined monster would look like, but not how I imagine it. And so forth. It appears in general that no one can argue that identity theory is not true because we know what our perceptions are like (or our emotions, and so on), and they are not at all like brain processes. That kind of self-knowledge almost certainly does not exist.

The same difficulty is encountered by some more formal disproofs. What the writer shows is that identity theory does not agree with some idea he has about mental activity, but these ideas are always theoretical ideas and not observable facts.

One writer says that a thought has no locus; since events in the brain obviously do have a locus, a thought cannot be a brain event. To prove that thoughts have no locus, he points out that it would not sound sensible to say that he had just had a thought at a particular point in space, perhaps halfway between his ears or two inches behind the bridge of his nose. The statement would sound silly indeed, but why? It is not that common sense is opposed to localization of thoughts, in view of such ordinary statements as "The idea never entered my head," or "He can't get it into his thick skull" that something or other is so. The reason it would be silly to say that I have a thought near my left ear may be merely that common sense sees no basis for saying just where in the skull a thought exists or perhaps would consider that it has volume instead of being punctate. But rejection by common sense, for whatever reason, proves nothing. Other fields of science are built on propositions that may seem absurd but in fact are true (air is heavy, has weight? water is made up of two gases? the continents are adrift in the oceans?). The idea that mental events have no locus (and perhaps that they are unextended) is really part of an older theory of the nature of the mind. As such it cannot disprove a later theory.

Another attempt at disproof: A writer says that mental events are private, known only to the person in whose mind they occur, whereas brain events are public, in principle observable by anyone; therefore a mental event cannot be a brain event. This apparently cogent argument has two flaws. One, it assumes that mental events are observable; two, it assumes that when something is known privately it cannot also be known publicly.

The example chosen in this case is pain, a favorite in such discussions perhaps because the term pain is ambiguous. It refers both to a distinctive sensation and to a resulting emotional state that tends to produce strong avoidance.[1] If we accept the example, the first point to note is that what a person in pain is directly aware of is not something in his mind, but something happening to or changed in his body. What he perceives is the pinprick or bruised shin or the state of affairs in and around his skull that he calls a

---

[1]Normally the two aspects of pain go together and are not distinguishable but they are separated in certain circumstances. The effect of morphine for example is mostly to reduce the unpleasantness of a pain rather than making the pain unrecognizable as such. Lobotomy for intractable pain does the same thing but more completely. The patient reports that the pain is the same as before—but it no longer bothers him.

headache. This perception is private, of course, but it is not introspective; one knows that one has burnt one's hand by the same sort of sensory process that lets one know that sandpaper is rough. The knowledge in short is perceptual, not introspective: It concerns something outside the mind, not inside. What the nature of the knowledge is is a theoretical problem, as concerns both sensation and the emotional reaction to the sensation. Neither can be examined directly to see what it is made of. Anyone who cares to make the observation will find that what he perceives when a hot iron touches his skin is something happening at that point; the perception is complicated by reflex withdrawal and by emotional reactions of avoidance, but the pain itself is perceived as being at the point of contact. The existence of the pain as a *mental* process is inferred. One cannot argue that the mental event is privately known, directly, and therefore that it cannot be a brain event since brain events are known publicly.

Thus the argument may be rejected simply because it assumes immediate experience of one's own mental activities. We can go further, however. Even if the student does not accept this—even if he holds to the existence of introspective knowledge—the argument has a second flaw. A privately known event can be known publicly at the same time. For example: When the skin is touched the fact is known privately, by sensation from the skin, but the same event can be known publicly by the subject himself as well as others, by means of vision. So even if the student does have private, direct knowledge of his own mental processes, that fact—if it is a fact—does not establish that the processes may not be detected by other (public) means. It is conceivable that when a person knows that he is afraid, privately, recording will become possible from electrodes in the limbic system of the brain, to make the same fact available publicly. That this should happen may not be probable or desirable, but the argument we are considering—the argument that mind cannot be a brain activity because one is known privately, the other publicly—is an argument in principle, and what I am showing here is that as such it does not hold water.

There are other disproofs that are no better. One says that the irreducibility of mind to brain is beautifully shown in the case of pain (that example again!) because there can be no pain without *awareness*. But this is to assume that awareness or consciousness is something different from brain function, which is exactly the point at issue. The question is begged completely.

Another attempt: If mind is a brain process, the writer says, we could not hear the clock strike twelve; the brain gets the same message twelve times, so, if that is all there is, what one would hear is the clock striking *one,* over and over. The fact that we actually hear it strike twelve means that there must be something else involved—namely, an immaterial mind—to count the strokes. This is an old argument but it has been repeated in recent years. It is an example of a certain tendency to base far-reaching philosophic conclusions on misinformation about the nervous system. When the brain is exposed to a series of stimulations, the stimuli may be identical but their effects in the brain are not. The state of the brain is modified by the first stimulus, which means that the impact of the second is different from that of the first. The third impact differs from the second in the same way, and it is easy to understand that the human subject may consequently become conditioned to say or think "one," "two," "three," and so on. There are of course theoretical problems about how such conditioning takes place but there is no doubt that it occurs and there is no logical requirement, consequently, of postulating something outside the nervous system to explain the phenomenon of counting. One's ability to hear the clock strike some number or other has nothing to do with the question whether the mind is a physical entity or not.

Although it is my personal conviction that mind and thought and consciousness *are* physical activities, functions of the brain, I have already said that this is a theory that cannot be proved. I am not foolish enough to attempt that logically impossible task. At most, one might at some time in the future show that all known mental phenomena are consistent with the theory, including some phenomena that are discovered as a result of working with the theory, but this would still fall short of establishing its truth. That is, there could be no way of showing that no one in the future would ever discover further phenomena that were incompatible with the theory.

A theory must be held tentatively, even after a long period of apparent confirmation. I have not tried to prove the truth of identity theory, only that it has not yet been disproved.

NONSENSE ABOUT BEHAVIORISM

Another impediment to understanding in this field is a common failure to see how the behavioristic emphasis in psychology came about, together with failure to understand the meaning of that term, behaviorism, which in some circles has become a term of abuse. For example, one writer, in discussing C. S. Peirce, goes out of his way to assure his readers that Peirce was not a behaviorist, though Peirce manifestly was one in an important sense, and this deprives Peirce of recognition for anticipating the logically behavioristic bias of modern psychology, including cognitive psychology. Others, psychologists among them, clearly regard behaviorism and John B. Watson as somehow beyond the pale, intellectually speaking, not fit topics for reasoned criticism. For them Watson was not only wrong, he was perversely wrong—a view that is itself perversely out of line with the facts and a prime example of that weakness in psychology and social science for adopting extreme positions in matters that call for a more discriminating judgement. Such a view of Watson would not survive if those who hold it would take the trouble to look into the record, instead of contenting themselves with second- and third-hand criticism.

In 1913, Watson did two things that must be distinguished if we are to understand his position. He proposed a general method for psychology, and he began the development of a theory to agree with it. The general method was behaviorism, requiring the use of objective evidence and denying the validity of introspection as a tool. Subsequent developments have shown that Watson was entirely right in this respect, as we will see in a moment, but, as the developments also showed, it took courage to make the point. The theory on the other hand was soon found to be defective, but it was not stupid and it had the immediate value of stimulating the research that led to its refutation and at the same time added to our understanding of human beings. In more than one way all psychologists, including those of us who disagree with his stimulus-response treatment of behavior, are in Watson's debt.

Consider first his methodological argument and the transformation of psychology into an objective science. The factual and theoretical developments in this century—which have changed the study of mind and behavior as radically as genetics changed the study of heredity—have all been the product of objective analysis—that is to say, behavioristic analysis. Thorndike, and later Skinner, on learning and reinforcement, Binet, and later Piaget, on the development of thought in childhood, Köhler on insight, Lashley on perception, Tolman on spatial orientation (the cognitive map), Beach on instinct as an aspect of intelligence (or vice versa), Lewin on leadership (making social psychology experimental in 1939), Harlow on cognitive motivation, Broadbent on the channeling of perception, and all the work in my laboratory showing the dependence of mind and thought on a close relation with the environment—all these and others based their conclusions on what the subjects did or said, and there is no nonbehavioristic study that ranks with them in importance.

Freud and the psychoanalysts are no exception. Rather the contrary, for Freud anticipated Watson in the actual use of behavioral evidence. His study of the unconscious is a most powerful argument that the mind cannot be known directly but must be approached inferentially; by definition the unconscious is not accessible to the subject's inspection, and another person—the analyst—may discover its content when the subject cannot. That contribution to method has been disregarded by the more biologically oriented psychologist. This is a pity, for there is an illuminating parallel with Darwin. Both men have profoundly changed the way we think about human beings, with a contribution that justifies calling them great men; and both have talked what we can now see is nonsense. Darwin established the fact of evolution and obliged us to see the fact of our close relation to other mammals, but in trying to justify his conclusions and show *how* evolution could work he also made ancillary hypotheses that are without value. For his part, Freud showed us the complexity of human motivation, the wide disorganization of thought and behavior that may result from a conflict with ideas deeply embedded during infancy, and really for the first time gave us some hint of the enormity of the problem of mind. But he also developed more specific propositions about infant ideas concerning sexual relations, for example, or the adult "determinism" that makes all forgetting motivated and all criticism malicious, which now look absurd. Like Darwin, Freud is entitled not to have his unconfirmed theoretical guesses held against him, obscuring the true contribution. We may add Freud's success to the evidence that accords with Watson's first main proposition, that psychology must function as an objective science.

If that methodological contribution were all, Watson could have escaped without scars. Instead, he went on to propose an unpalatable theory. It was not merely unpalatable, it was outrageous for most of his contemporaries, but as it happened it was not one that his critics could refute offhand by reasoned argument. The result was that some of them resorted to ridicule. Broad for example said something to the effect that Watson must be very intelligent, for only an intelligent man could be so stupid. There was no need of showing flaws in the theory; it was *obviously* wrong, and this attitude toward "behaviorism" persists today in large areas of social science as well as psychology and philosophy. Outrageous Watson may have been in treating mind as a myth and images and ideas as mere misleading verbal habits, but he had a solid scientific basis for that view—the neurophysiology of the day denied the possibility of any activity of the brain other than sensorimotor transmissions. There was no holding or reworking of sensory input, no interaction between inputs, no output originating in the brain itself, according to existing anatomical and physiological knowledge. One would think that any philosopher of science who respects logic would also respect Watson for basing theory on the facts at his disposal and not on tradition or personal preference. Unfortunately for Watson, the facts were wrong—at best incomplete—but it was only in 1938, 25 years later, that this was finally established by Lorente de Nó, and only in 1940 that the changed situation was brought to the attention of the psychological world by Hilgard and Marquis (1940), in a brief reference to the possibility of the brain's holding input before transmitting it to the muscles. Meanwhile, psychologists had been attacking Watson's theory by experimental means, beginning with Hunter's (1913) demonstration of delayed response in Harvey Carr's laboratory at Chicago, which showed that raccoons and children possessed a kind of cognitive function that Watson's theory denied them. We will return to this topic in discussing the evolution of mind and thought (Chapter 4); I mention it here to contrast such criticism, by logical analysis and the obtaining of new evidence, with criticism by contemptuous comment. John B. Watson was not a fool, the objectivity he imposed on psychological method is the basis of a great advance in knowledge, and his relatively primitive theory was in fact hard to disprove conclusively. "Behaviorism" is not synonymous with any particular theory of behavior; Lashley and Tolman both called themselves behaviorists, though each of them spent the better part of his career showing the inadequacy of the particular theory of behavior that Watson had proposed. Lashley's avowed object was to understand the mind, stated in those words; Tolman avoided the term mind, but that was what he was working on in showing that cognitive functions can be detected even in the laboratory rat.

B. F. Skinner is the modern representative of much that Watson stood for, and criticism of his work has taken much the same course. He is a brilliant experimentalist with a record of valuable contributions to human welfare, a fact that one would not detect from the kind of comment made in the journals of social science. One may well disagree with his radical positivism and the theoretcial narrowness that results, as I do, but this should not blind the critic to the fact of the outstanding contribution. It is astonishing that the proposal of *Beyond Freedom and Dignity* (Skinner, 1971) to substitute positive reward for punishment and make criminals not want to be criminals should have appeared to a wide range of social scientists as a vicious program of thought control. Moderation is possible in all things, and there is nothing about a program of modification of one kind of behavior that says it must be applied to all other behavior. In fact, as Skinner himself remarked, his proposal was not practical; and if it is impractical to control criminal behavior and aggression by making use of (anticipatory) reinforcements, it is ten times more so to establish a control of all other aspects of behavior, throughout society. Skinner's discussion was academic, in both senses of the word, an expression of a concern for practical problems that has appeared in his work on human learning and in the work of his students and other likeminded colleagues with patients in the back wards of mental hospitals, or behavior modification in minor psychopathologies. Programmed learning is not a substitute for teaching, but a valuable tool for the teacher's use where rote learning is concerned. Behavior modification is not a cure for psychosis and not even for neurosis, but still there are crippling deviations from normal behavior that it can deal with better than other kinds of psychotherapy. A particular case is stuttering, the treatment of which has been very greatly improved by the systematic application of—essentially—Skinnerian methods. Some of Skinner's views may be wrong, in principle, but in practice they have been brilliantly successful, with a more valuable contribution to society than those of any of his social-science critics.

To talk of behaviorism as blind incompetence is ignorance or prejudice or both. It is certainly not a mark of scholarship.

PSYCHOLOGY AND HUMANISM

The transformation of psychology into a biological science has had a narrowing effect, because science generally is self-limiting. Its power depends entirely on working only with problems for which adequate data and methods are available. Even speculation must stay within sight of the data and is taken seriously only with the background assumption that methods of testing if not available now may possibly show up in the future. One of the first things the neophyte researcher must learn is to cut his coat to suit his cloth, to put on his pants one leg at a time (Ivan Petrovich Pavlov's advice!), not bite off bigger pieces than he can chew: in other words, not to pick the most important problem for research but the most important problem for which the tools are available and a method he can handle, with the expectation that when the first step has been taken he will be better able to see how to take the next. It is this step by step advance that has revolutionized psychology and made it productive of new knowledge and new understanding. But at the same time it has set to one side some of the most interesting and significant features of human behavior as not suitable for scientific investigation, at least for the present and perhaps forever.

The resulting situation has been most unsatisfactory to many, psychologists and others, who have felt that as psychology was becoming scientific in its methods, it became less relevant to human problems. They may not have thought in those terms. They may not blame the narrowness on science—science is supposed to be the answer to all difficulties, so how is one to attribute psychology's shortcomings to its being scientific? But there was *something* wrong, and the cure proposed was to make psychology *more* scientific by having it turn to those important problems that were being forgotten—in the jargon of the day, make psychology relevant. This is more or less what humanistic psychology amounts to. The important human problems are ones that have always been the concern of the humanities, so the whole idea comes down to having psychology take over the domain of literature or large parts of it.

But this is to have your cake and eat it too. The breadth of the humanities is beyond the scope of science. The narrowness of scientific method with its insistence on the formal specification of data and how they relate to the conclusions must stifle the spirit of literature, and proposing that psychology should pick its problems on the basis of their social importance instead of the feasibility of attack must equally stultify research.

All this somehow undervalues the humanities, as if we psychologists could do the job better. Scientific knowledge, resulting from experiment and formal analysis, tends to be surer but it also tends to be molecular, and it is not necessarily truer or better than the more molar knowledge of the nonscientific observer. Scientific psychology is steadily increasing its scope and we can expect that its "relevance" will increase likewise, so it needs no justification for continuing on its narrow path—narrow at present, but becoming less and less so—and it may some day begin to rival the accumulated wisdom of human experience. But it has not got there yet and can only hope to do so by going its own way, shortsighted as it may often be.

Thus my argument does not derogate the humanities or humanism, but the contrary. Science as applied to human behavior is not yet ready to replace the wisdom of the great teachers, nor even the ordinary good literature of the novelist, dramatist, poet or biographer who may fall short of genius but still has something to show us about human behavior, even when his or her name is not one of the great ones. Modesty still becomes us. Psychology has indeed shown that it is on its way, already with significant contributions to human wisdom, but—as above—it is not about to replace good literature and be a sole source of the understanding of man.

SCIENCE AND COMMON SENSE

Now to return to that question of common sense and to see why, valuable as it is, it can have no casting vote when it opposes scientific theory; in the present case specifically, the theory that awareness consists of—not merely accompanies, but *is*—some pattern of nerve impulses running to and fro in the brain.

In his campaign to educate the Victorian public in support of Darwin's theory of evolution, T.H. Huxley once referred to science as organized common sense. This may have been effective propaganda but it was not a complete description: up to a point, sound enough, but in important respects we can much better see common sense as a continuing target of science, slowly changing under the impact of new discoveries. Common sense largely derives from our common human experience but it also includes scientific ideas when they have aged well and become familiar. The process of incorporating such ideas may take 50 to 100 years or even more—and getting rid of them another 100 when they turn out later to have been scientific mistakes. Everyone today knows why we breathe; the need of oxygen is a matter of common sense, though once the whole question was deeply puzzling to Samuel Pepys and his brilliant friends of Royal Society.[2] The circulation of the blood is a familiar common-sense idea, and so are the ideas of air pressure, of gravity, of electrical charge and electrical current or resistance, and of acidity; and all these features of common-sense knowledge are direct products of science. On

---

[2]See Pepys' *Diary* for January 22, 1665. It was more than 100 years later that Lavoisier found the explanation, as a by-product of his oxygen theory of combustion.

the other hand, this is the same common sense that once knew that a heavy body falls faster than a lighter one, that the stars revolve about the earth, that nature abhors a vacuum, that a receding chin shows a weakness of personality, and that genius is a close relative of insanity. Some of these wrong ideas came from science too, and were only slowly replaced by later ones. As a mixture of ancient theory and various generalizations from human experience, common sense is often right—but not always. An appeal to what everyone knows, or pointing out that any sensible person would regard a proposition as absurd, cannot be valid objections to the scientific idea that works well in other respects. This is particularly true of the new idea, or an old one in new form; for it is likely, as it becomes more familiar, to seem obvious to common sense and become generally accepted.

Ideas now commonplace were often enough unacceptable when first proposed, and it may not be realized how peculiar some of the conceptions are that made possible the great advances of modern science. For most of us modern physics has become unintelligible, and physicists may encourage this attitude by saying that their ideas can only be understood in mathematical terms. But these ideas can be communicated in words, roughly and in part, and when they are they turn out to be very peculiar. The ether has been abolished, but electrons and positrons and so forth, besides being particles, are also waves—though now there is nothing for them to be waves of, or in. Here common sense must object; but the theory is abundantly supported by experimental fact. Another surprising conception is that of antimatter: The electron, with a negative charge, is part of ordinary matter, the positron with positive charge is antimatter. Both are forms of energy, fundamentally, thus striking directly at any common sense conception of matter as an inert filler of space to be contrasted with the pure immaterial energy of mind.

Physics of course is logical, as a science must be, but not in any ordinary way. Some time ago it appeared that theory and observation were on a collision course, for well-established and valuable conceptions were contradicted by the results of nuclear experiment. What to do, when fact and theory differ? What we are taught is, reject the theory: Common sense as well as logic would say the same thing, for theory is only speculation and cannot oppose fact. But physics said Nonsense, it is perfectly good theory, and on the spot invented the neutrino—a new particle, but one with no mass and not even an electric charge to make it detectable, a surprising conception indeed. Without it, however, an equation would not balance and the law of the conservation of mass-energy would be endangered, so it must exist.

As it turned out the neutrino found other support (more or less of the same kind) and is at present solidly established in the conceptual armamentarium of physics. None of this makes light of physical science, which has provided plenty of evidence to show that its modes of thought are sound: evidence not only in the control of nuclear energy but in radar, television from the moon, and the many chemical products that also contribute to the current revolution in human existence. What I do here is simply remind the reader of how far science may get from ordinary common sense.

And mathematics too, which of course is deeply involved in the operations of science. Mathematics for example first established that the square root of a minus quantity is nonexistent and, for ordinary people, a meaningless conception; it then goes on to make i, the square root of minus one, a fundamentally important building block in higher mathematical operations; or having developed a conception of infinity as without limit in size, than which one would think there can be nothing greater, it then allows and even encourages Georg Cantor to develop the notion of a series of infinities of which *aleph sub zero* is ordinary infinity, *aleph sub one* a bigger infinity, and so on.

It may seem, if these forms of thought are surprising, that it is only our unsophistication as laymen that makes them unusual. It is therefore worth noting that mathematicians and scientists themselves have felt on occasion that things were getting out of hand. According to Hadamard (1954), Cantor's theory of sets, now a fundamental part of mathematics, seemed at first so paradoxical and so inconsistent with accepted ideas that another eminent mathematician managed to prevent Cantor from getting any new appointment and even from publishing in German journals. Barber (1961) has discussed the great men of science, themselves originators of new ideas, who were unable to stomach the new ideas of others. Yet these are ideas that, properly aged, are now solidly established as scientific truth. Lord Kelvin regarded Röntgen's x–rays as a hoax, refused to accept Rutherford's planetary model of the atom, and refused also to accept Maxwell's electromagnetic theory of light because he could not make a common-sense mechanical model to correspond. Galileo laughed at Kepler's idea that the ocean is attracted by the moon, to account for the tides. In biological science Pasteur's theory of disease, like Semmelweiss's ideas about antisepsis, was violently resisted; Darwin was rejected not only by churchmen but also by Owen and Agassiz and other scientists; and Gregor Mendel was rejected by everyone, partly it seems on the ground that mathematics can have no place in the study of botany.

The new idea that requires any great revision of existing thought may seem outrageous, and not only to common sense, until the new way of thinking has become familiar. Eventually it may become as "obvious" to common sense as the Copernican and Newtonian theory of planetary motion, or the theory of evolution, is today; and in judging current scientific thought it is well to recall these aspects of its development in the past.

The psychological idea that an awareness of one's environment, or a feeling of sadness, or a memory, consists of a pattern of nerve impulses—this is not on the face of it a plausible idea at all. But that is not a test of its scientific validity. Other implausible ideas—for example, that the moon exerts an attraction on the ocean, that matter and energy are the same thing—have with exposure become more acceptable, and have also been the keys to great advances of knowledge. The idea that brain and mind are one may have a similar future.

It should be observed that accepting biological theory as a working hypothesis commits one to no belief. The theory may even be accepted with the ultimate purpose of showing its inadequacy, thus supporting the alternative animistic theory of an immaterial mind or soul. The logic is clear. Suppose that one day the theory of the mind as brain function is fully developed and that there then remain some aspects of human experience and behavior that are not accounted for. In such a case we would have a demonstration that in man we are dealing with something more than a physiological organism. It will be a long time in the future before such a stage of knowledge will be possible, and it is still a question whether science will ever master the appalling complexities of brain function, so this may seem a very academic point, of no present significance. But it does have significance in showing how, logically, one may work with one theory *because* one believes in another.

This is the *reductio ad absurdum* of Euclid: to prove that two sides of a triangle are equal, assume that they are not—and show that the assumption results in absurdity, thus proving what it was desired to prove in the first place. It is the *null hypothesis* of statistics: to show that two samples are "significantly different" and must have come from two populations, assume that they came from one—and then show how improbable this is. Similarly, to show that there is a soul that is not part of the body's activities, assume that there is not one, with the hope or expectation that the assumption will eventually be found insufficient.

There is no theory of mind or behavior that has not grave defects, of incompleteness and probable error. It is reasonable to have a preference and even to believe either that there is a soul or that there is not; but in the present state of knowledge it is not reasonable to be dogmatic either way, and it is especially not reasonable to object to working with the biological theory of mind on the ground that one does not believe it. This is like refusing in statistics to set up the null hypothesis because one believes it is not true, which is absurd: The purpose of setting it up is to disprove it. The biological theory has been the fertile one in this century. If it is untrue it may have a function like that of Newton's theory of absolute space, which permitted a development of physics that eventually led Einstein to see how to destroy the theory and replace it with a better one. In psychology today it is the biological approach that has been increasing our knowledge and comprehension of human beings; it may be implausible to say that consciousness consists of a biochemical activity of a multitude of nerve impulses traversing pathways in the brain but it nevertheless begins to look very much as though the proposition is true. It is at least a good working assumption.

2 Self-Knowledge and the Self

In any discussion of the nature of mind or the relation of mind to body, a crucial point always lies in the question whether one knows one's mind directly. There is always an argument against identifying mental processes with activity of the brain that runs like this: I *know* what my mind is like, and it is not like what that identification implies; mind is totally unlike any physical process. If however one does not have that direct unassailable knowledge, if one's information about the mind is a matter of inference and theory, then the issue becomes a choice between two sets of theoretical ideas by the sole criterion of their relative effectiveness. Here we will first see what reason there is for doubting that introspection—*immediate* self-knowledge or self-observation by the mind [3]—exists. But the idea that it does exist is deep-seated, and the argument may be more convincing if we can see how such a mistaken idea might have come about.

A further point is this. One does after all know something of what is going on in one's mind at any particular time, and until one can explain that fact it must constitute a strong argument in favor of the existence of introspection. If one's self-knowledge is inferential, how is the inference made? Closely related is the idea of an observing self. In all this there are some surprising

---

[3] "Introspection" is often used loosely to include any form of private knowledge, such as sensation of muscle tension, or imagery. As we will see, even imagery is an outward-looking mechanism, not inward-looking; and muscle sensation, though it is private, is as objective in mechanism as seeing a cow or hearing a horn. As a technical term, *introspection* is direct observation by the mind of its own activity. The whole question is whether the mind can know itself in such an inward way with no intervention of a sensory process.

phenomena which may be particularly interesting when considered from the point of view of a biological theory of mind.

INTROSPECTION: HISTORICAL METAPHOR?

It is only in the modern period, from John Locke onward, that philosopher-psychologists have made explicit the view that the way the mind is to be investigated must be by self-observation. It was even later—200 years later, toward the end of the 19th century—that the first rigorous attempt to do so was made by Wilhelm Wundt; in the meantime everyone apparently took it for granted that this was how psychologists were operating, but it was only in Wundt's laboratory that the method was actually tried. Of course, Descartes used his knowledge of his own thought in theoretical discussion, but there is little indication of how he got the knowledge. Locke made it explicit: The mind knows itself directly.

How it knows itself was a problem, one that reappears in the discussions of later writers, but we can see how the matter must have appeared to Locke. Obviously one knows what one is thinking of, much of the time, and how can that be otherwise than by—somehow—observing those thoughts? We usually regard our information about anything as the result of observing it or being told about it, forgetting how much is inferential even in everyday matters; here there is no question of being told about one's thoughts, so they must somehow be observed. Also, Locke wrote at a time when certain Cartesian ideas were still being absorbed, concerning mind as an entity cut off from the external world by the intervention of the sensory pathways (ideas that Berkeley would soon develop further). Any mechanism of inference that depended on sensation would be neither obvious nor plausible as a means by which the mind could learn of itself.

So it seemed that the mind must know itself directly, and as Ryle (1949) remarked, Locke found a convenient analogy with looking in a mirror. The mind might somehow *reflect* on itself. This figure of speech became common property in the next hundred years, "reflection" becoming a synonym for thought (as it still is). In such use by the layman the term lost all its special significance. Some more specialized (and more impressive?) word was needed by the philosopher-psychologist, and that need was met by "introspection," about 1800. Introspection, looking inward, is still a figure of speech and if anything worse in its effect on psychological thought. It is easier to develop a fantasy about the mind looking inward than of the mind using a looking-glass and furthermore to forget that it *is* fantasy.

In this approach to mind, a fundamental limitation was encountered early. All that could be found, in self-examination, was mental content, with no sign of a self to do the knowing. David Hume's experience was that he seemed never to find anything but "some particular perception or other." This limitation on reflection or introspection became even more restrictive in the work of the empiricists and "British associationists" (not all British) of the 19th century. Instead of perceptions they found only sensations: thus Wundt and his eminent student and contemporary E. B. Titchener of Cornell. It then appeared that mental content is made up entirely of sensations and images (internally arising sensations). Since these were observable it could be supposed that the whole mind lay open to introspection—and an incredibly shallow, flat and unconvincing mind it was, as it appears in the research of this whole school of thought.

It is absolutely essential for anyone today who wants psychology to return to the subjective method of an earlier day, regarded as less narrow and closer to the reality of the human mind, to realize that the experts at the time of the highest development of subjective method, between say 1880 and 1910, were agreed that it could find nothing but sensory content. The resulting psychology was barren beyond belief—exactly what William James was complaining about in 1890 in *The Principles of Psychology*. It was just in this period that Sigmund Freud was beginning to reveal complexities that were hidden from the introspectionists, but it was another twenty or thirty years before his work had much impact on the psychologists of the academic world. In the meantime Alfred Binet and Oswald Külpe were getting experimental results that pointed in the same direction, though their full significance was not apparent till much later: Binet, in fact, has never been recognized for his discoveries in this part of his many-sided research.

Külpe worked with doctoral students at Würzburg—the "Würzburg School"—for a ten-year period beginning in 1900. In general terms, Binet and Külpe showed the existence of mental activity that could not be found by introspection, at about the same time as Freud, although there was no connection at all between the two lines of research. Freud called this activity the unconscious, Külpe called it imageless thought. "Imageless thought" looked like nonsense to most psychologists, who were sure that thought was made up of images, only, and these results were vehemently rejected by the orthodox.

One experimental result in particular will show what it was that was so upsetting. Külpe had proposed to introspect on thought in action instead of looking only at the elements of thought as others were doing. In this experiment the subject was given simple arithmetical operations to perform, the idea being that he should introspect at the same time. He was shown pairs of digits such as 6 and 4, 7 and 2, 5 and 3, for addition at one time, and at a different time for subtraction or multiplication. After the subject was well into one of these series of operations, however, he was surprised to find no evidence at all of any accompanying thought. He saw the pair of digits and had the answer, nothing more. Now this is still a surprising result. Presented with a 6 and a 4 the subject had the answer *ten* when he was doing a series of additions; but doing a series of subtractions he had the answer *two*. The given numbers, the stimulus combination, were the same; what made the difference in the response? At the time it was expected perhaps that there would also be imagery of the word *add* in one case, *subtract* in the other. Thus: 6, 4, *add;* or 6, 4, *subtract*. Nothing of the sort was found. The subject was just "set" to add or to subtract, and the nature of the set was not evident. Something else was going on in the mind and it did not consist of images, which the subject would have been able to report.

The demonstration of imageless thought made a radical qualification of what one could hope for from introspection. Hume had limited its possibilities to the study of sensory content, and now Külpe showed that these reportable sensory elements were not after all the whole story of mental activity. There are things going on in one's mind that are not introspectable at all.

The final step in this progressive limitation of the role of introspection in psychological research was to reduce it to zero. George Humphrey in his book *Thinking* (1951) showed that when the classical introspectors at Cornell thought they were describing a sensation they were really describing the external event or object that had given rise to the sensation. He generalized his conclusions as follows—tentatively, it is true, but the case he made was convincing and has not been refuted: *"We perceive objects directly, not through the intermediary of 'presentations,' 'ideas,' or 'sensations.'* Similarly, *we imagine objects directly,* not through the intermediary of images, though images are present as an important part of the whole activity" (p. 129). What one is aware of in perception is not a percept but the object that is perceived; what is given in imagination is an illusory external object, not an internal mental representation called an image. This latter notion and the percept are inferred (but they undoubtedly exist, as atoms do likewise.)

Others have come to the same conclusion. Humphrey has the special importance of having shown why what seemed to be introspection was in fact something else, even in the case of the trained introspectors of Cornell under the eye of E.B. Titchener. E.G. Boring's (1953) agreement with Humphrey must carry weight also, since he was originally trained by Titchener; and C. S. Peirce, America's greatest philosopher, came to the same conclusion a hundred years ago, although in this, as in other respects, he was so far ahead of his time that what he had to say was apparently not heard at all.

THE PARADOXICAL UNCONSCIOUS

Currently being incorporated into the body of common-sense knowledge is the existence of what is known as the unconscious. The idea originated with Herbart, early in the 19th century, but is now principally associated with Freud and Jung. It is correspondingly popular in the literary world, with the idea apparently that all human motivation is darkly Freudian, but also that creativity and genius reside in this so-to-speak "basement" of the mind. And herein lies a paradox, as K.S. Lashley once observed. He pointed out that there is no *conscious* mind (in the Freudian and Jungian sense), and consequently that the behavior of conscious man, in his normal waking state, is all determined by his unconscious. For the unconscious is the mental activity that is not open to observation, not introspectable, and this as we have just seen is true of *all* mental activity. The conclusion one must draw, then, is that *the unconscious comprises the whole mind.* We have lost, in making psychology an objective study, not the unconscious but consciousness.

The paradox of course is easily resolved. It is simply the result of using the term conscious in two very different senses. In the first it denotes one state of a human being, in the second it denotes a restricted segment of mental activity. The primary reference of the word "conscious" is to the condition of a normal waking adult, one who is conscious of and responsive to his environment. Herbart changed that meaning completely when he used the term to designate those ideas of which—he considered—he was conscious. The first meaning refers to one who is aware of things; the second refers to something that he is aware of, or thinks he is.

Here we have an excellent example of the relation between common sense and technical ideas, which common sense slowly absorbs and equally slowly excretes when they turn out to be ill-founded. It is only in the past 20 years or so that this idea of the unconscious has reached its present peak of popularity: 50 or 60 years after Freud, 150 after Herbart, and just at the time when the technical evidence calls for considerable change. It is now becoming clear that most of Freud's more adventurous specific hypotheses lack factual support. It is these that are particularly attractive in the world of literature and literary criticism, with little awareness of his less dramatic but truly fundamental insights. It is also clear, as I have tried to show in the preceding pages, that we can no longer conceive of the unconscious as a deep well in which the conscious may fish—for there is no conscious to do the fishing and the unconscious, illogically named, is the sole seat of consciousness.

Here it is important to note that the unconscious does not deal only in unpleasant, guilt-provoking ideas. The clear experimental evidence is provided by Külpe, who as we have seen showed that ideas as simple and guilt-free as those of elementary arithmetic may be unreportable. They too are "unconscious" and are known only by inference. This more benign aspect of the so-called unconscious has been emphasized and broadened by recent discussions of creativity, beginning apparently with the reports of his discoveries by the great French mathematician, Henri Poincaré, elaborated by Hadamard (1954). Much of the dramatic in such reports disappears when we realize that what they mean is not that there is a strange creative entity within us foreign to our true ("conscious") nature, but simply that our thought, creative or not, is not open to our observation and may on occasion come up with conclusions that surprise. It is one's own mind that is strange, creative and unknown, a genuine mystery.

THE SPECIAL CASE OF
IMAGERY AND HALLUCINATION

To the reader it may have seemed a contradiction to talk about images while at the same time denying the existence of introspection. What else is it when I report having an image of something or other? The something or other is not present, so the image is in my mind, so I am describing mental content when I describe it; and that is introspection. A reply is already available in the quotation from Humphrey above: What one is describing is an illusory external object, not the mental activity. However, all this is a very different way of thinking about mental processes and we must go into it in more detail. The traditional way of thinking is long established and deeply ingrained, and one may with some difficulty have to learn to think differently.

The first important point is that the term "image" is used in two ways, one of them misleading; at least, it is certainly misleading to use the word in two quite different senses without realizing the fact. One meaning is a reference to the imagined object or event that seems to be seen or heard or felt. The other refers to the internal process, the reason why I seem to be seeing or hearing or feeling. To take a simple example, I stare at a bright light for a few seconds and then look away at a blank surface. On the surface appears a dark spot. This may be referred to as an image, since its transience and the fact that it moves as my eyes move tell me that there is no spot there; what I seem to see is the result of something happening in me, in my visual system. But that something happening inside may *also* be referred to as an image, and the two conceptions are fundamentally different. We must not use the same technical term to refer both to the illusory outside event and the real but theoretical one inside. Which meaning we should retain is not important logically, but one of them—the one that makes imagery a mental activity— is well established and not likely to change, so it is the other that we should abandon. I propose then the following terminology: In the situation described, I *have* an image (a mental activity not observable); what I *see* (and can describe) is an (illusory) spot on the surface that I am looking at.

This way of speaking may seem more sensible if we think of the physiological basis of the imagery. In the case of the after-image just referred to, as one looks away from the bright light some sensory cells are fatigued and there is a rebound effect in others whose activity was suppressed; the result is that when one looks at the blank surface there is an actual sensory activity

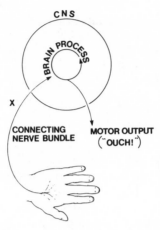

FIG. 1. Schematizing the phantom limb. Sensation from the hand normally depends on connecting nerves, but if the arm is amputated and the neural connection cut at X, spontaneous activity in the remaining part of the nerve bundle will continue to deliver sensory messages to the brain. Pain may be perceived and responded to normally, in this abnormal situation.

corresponding to seeing a dark area surrounded by a lighter one. In this sense one really does see a dark spot whose size, shape and locus can be described, in the same way as when there is a spot that others can see as well.

Another illustrative example is provided by the phantom limb, a hallucination[4] that is a result, apparently in every case, of surgical amputation. After an arm has been cut off the patient continues to have somesthetic awareness of it, so convincing that as he recovers, lying in bed after the operation with the stump covered by the bedclothes, he may think that the surgeon changed his mind and did not operate after all. In a certain proportion of cases, perhaps 15%, the patient also has pain. He may report cramps and describe a twisted-up posture of the missing limb. Note however that what he can describe is a twisted limb just as, in the case of the after-image, it was the (nonexistent) spot on the wall that could be described and not the sensory basis of seeing it. Complaining of pain in the phantom is not a report of introspection but reaction to a sensory process that has got out of order.

Figure 1 schematically shows a hand normally connected with the brain and the speech apparatus. If this hand is pinched the subject says "Ouch!"; sensory pathways from the skin carry excitation to the brain, which excites the central processes that constitute pain, and these excite motor outflow to

---

[4]"Hallucination" may be used to mean only the imagery that deceives, when the subject thinks he is perceiving and not imagining; or it may be used to refer to imagery that is in itself convincing, though there may be other evidence to show that it is illusory. The latter usage is better. After amputation of a leg, the persisting phantom is convincing; the amputee recovering consciousness after operation may think that the surgeon changed his mind and did not cut—till he sees the stump. He then has a hallucination by the first definition. But the phantom-process is not changed by that further information, so it deserves the same designation. See Siegel and West (1975).

the speech organs. No introspection is involved. In principle this is a motor response to external stimulation. A sensory input causes a motor output; no question arises of any need of self-contemplation by the mind to account for the behavior.

Now consider the situation when that hand is amputated. Pain stimulation beginning in the hand is no longer possible, but the same sort of message may reach the brain even though it begins at a higher point in the sensory pathway, perhaps at the point X in Figure 1. If nerve cells are not regularly excited by external stimulation they tend to fire spontaneously. If now the patient who has lost the hand still says *"Ouch,"* or *"I have a pain in my hand"* the mechanism—at the level of the brain—is exactly the same one as before. There is still no question of introspection.

A memory image may be regarded in much the same way. It is a reinstatement of perceptual activity either as a result of spontaneous firing in the neurons that make it up, or by its being excited associatively, by some other central activity. This is represented in Figure 2. You see something unusual in the microscope, let us say, and describe it so your laboratory partner will be able to identify it when he or she has his or her turn at the eyepiece. The visual sensory input excites a brain process that in turn excites the motor output of speech; later, talking to some other student, something you think of reminds you of what you saw and you can describe it again. It is shown in Figure 2 that there is no need to raise any question of the mind examining itself when such a case of imagery occurs. When the perception is reinstated by means of an association with some other mental process ("central excitant" in the figure) this amounts to a kind of short-circuiting of response to the environment.

Whether the mind has immediate self-knowledge or not—whether or not Peirce and Humphrey and Boring are wrong in denying it—it is at least clear that one's ability to report imagery and to describe what one seems to see (or hear or feel) does not consitute crucial evidence in support of the subjective approach to the study of mind.

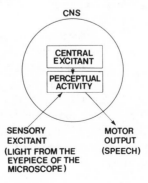

FIG. 2. A "perceptual activity" may be excited by sensation, as when a student sees something in the microscope. This is perception. But it may also be excited by a connection with some other mental event ("central excitant"). Then it is a memory image, which can cause the same verbal response as the original perception.

THE IDEA OF THE SELF

So far this discussion has been negative, attempting to show that a truly subjective psychology is not possible; at the least, that it is not logically unavoidable. In doing so, it may have given the impression that objective psychology leads to over-simplification. Nothing could be farther from the truth, as we will now see. Looking at ideas of oneself lands us immediately in great complexities.

My first proposition is that *the idea of the self* and *the idea of the other* overlap, have a part in common, and that this accounts for the existence of empathy and certain related phenomena.

Let us begin by asking how the idea of the self might develop in infancy. The baby has a great handicap in regard to himself, for he lacks perspective. He can see some parts of himself, but his body of course is not visible as a whole (unless he sits or stands before a mirror, and even here there are limits). On the other hand he has frequent opportunity to observe others walking, approaching or retreating, standing erect or bending over and, just as important, all the transitions from one of these postures to another. It seems therefore that the child's idea of a person must first come from his observation of others. Instead of knowing himself first and inferring that others are like him he may reverse that order and, observing the similarity of his own hand and foot and their activities and his vocalization to the hands and feet and vocalizations of others, gradually develop an idea of himself that is in the first place the idea of a *person,* only secondarily an idea of *this person.* In the theory of brain function that is presented later, in Chapter 6, any but the very simplest idea is a complex, and what I am proposing here is that the child develops a complex idea of a person, together with ancillary qualifying part-ideas that specify which or what kind of person (mother, woman, boy, etc.). In the present case, person plus one qualifying part-idea is the *other,* person plus a different qualifying part-idea is the *self.*

Direct and compelling support for such a conception is provided by a personal experience of my own. At the age of 26 an infection resulted in the complete immobilization of my right hip. When I got on my feet again I had to learn some new patterns of behavior. Being unable to bend in the middle I could sit down only with some support, putting a hand on the arm of the chair or the back of the couch to lower myself into it. I was completely unaware of how deep the learning had sunk in until one day a friend at a party walked up to a Chesterfield, bent in the middle, and sat—a totally impossible action. The sight was astonishing, though it took only a second or two to return to reality and see that it was only I who could not sit down so. The same experience recurred once or twice in the following months and then disappeared, as I apparently distinguished more effectively between *self* and *other.* I am still not sure however that the distinction was complete; for some years later when

I had occasion to remind myself of the earlier experience, thus making the circumstances vivid in memory, I had the experience once more, with the same sudden astonishment followed by realization of the separation between self and other.

Now there appears to be no other explanation of this experience than by supposing that the idea of the self and the idea of the other have a common element. The explanation also gets a certain support from the phenomena of empathy—which is seen even in chimpanzees. Köhler (1927) has published a fascinating photograph of one of his chimpanzees showing an empathic identification with another. The second animal, whose task is to reach a banana hung high up, stands on a precarious structure of boxes piled on one another and stretches for the prize now barely within reach: at which point the first animal, who has already solved the problem and is now made to sit to one side and look on, reaches upward with his arm at the same time and in the same posture. His idea, his expectation, of the other's action produces the same action in himself.

A certain degree of support is also provided by a more or less common human experience. Trying to get a reluctant year-old baby to accept a spoonful of mush—that is, trying to get the baby to open a mouth so the spoon can be inserted—inevitably results in opening one's own mouth, much as one feels like a fool in doing so. Observations made in a children's hospital where parents visit and sometimes are allowed to feed their own infants show that mothers are less vulnerable to this effect (presumably because they have had more opportunity to develop an inhibition); fathers are quite unable to keep their mouths shut. The idea of another opening his mouth—concentrating on that idea to the exclusion of anything else—produces the same movement in oneself. Since no other explanantion of empathy, altruism and imitation generally is available, all these facts support the notion that one's idea of oneself and one's idea of another share the common idea of a person. The proposal is Woodworth's (1938) "schema with correction": The schema in this case is the basic idea of a person, the correction is the qualifying ancillary part-idea that makes the whole represent a particular person.

This line of thought introduces a fundamental objectivity into the idea of the self, like a stranger permanently in the home. It brings us also to a fundamental creativity about the image which is quite inconsistent with the age-old conception of an image as simply a reinstatement of some particular perceptual event. The elements indeed must have a perceptual origin, but the whole gestalt may do more than merely reassemble them unchanged, and even the memory image may incorporate a significant creativity.

Let us look at this property of the image, for it directly concerns ideas of the self. A simple example first. Some time ago I realized with surprise that some of my visual "memories" were of places and things seen from a new angle—that is, from a point in space at which I had never been. I have a vivid memory for example of a certain field known in childhood, but as seen from a point some thirty feet in the air from which all corners of the field would be visible—not true of any one point on the ground. Others have comparable experiences, commonly in recalling the countryside or the city in which they live: Here one may mix up true memory images—recall of something as actually seen—with the effects of having seen a map.

We now know also that much more dramatic forms of imagery are possible, apart from dreaming—that is, in a waking state, when one's behavior appears normal—and in circumstances that are also normal apart from a prolonged monotony which appears to contribute to the effect. The experimental subjects in isolation (p. 96) saw, among other things, primitive animals in a prehistoric jungle and modern squirrels wearing snowshoes. A test pilot at 60,000 feet began to feel that his plane was a toy balanced on a pin, and saw himself from outside like a puppet at the controls (Hebb, 1960). At such an altitude the ground below may take on a monotonous sameness. The ocean does the same from lower altitudes, and Charles Lindbergh (1953) in his solitary flight across the Atlantic was aware of "ghostly presences riding in my airplane" and "vapor-like shapes crowding the fuselage, speaking with human voices, giving me advice and important messages." Solitary sailors, and survivors of shipwreck in lifeboats, report having visions. Even on land, in apparently normal circumstances, the monotony of long-distance car-driving on the Western plains of the North American continent may lead the driver to see things—jackrabbits big enough to step over the car in one case—and the long-distance truck-driver at night following that endless white line down the highway may wreck his truck trying to avoid collision with a nonexistent object on the highway before him.

This creativity becomes directly relevant to our present concerns when it involves imagery of one's own body. An example is the test pilot who saw himself at the controls of his own plane. Another example, it seems clear, is the student in the isolation experiment who reported that his mind seemed like a ball of cotton wool above where his body lay in the experimental cubicle (not to mention the report of another that he had two bodies and was unsure which was his own, or the one who said that his head seemed to be detached from his neck). The mind separate from the body of course reminds us of the occasional reports of mystics who can detach the mind at will and the mystically-minded laymen to whom this happens like a rare and exciting event. For these persons the mind really leaves the body, but there is a less radical explanation. I do not try to show that they are necessarily wrong—I have already said that there is no way of disproving the existence of a noncorporeal mind (which might indeed be inclined to wander)—but I do propose that a better explanation is simply the occurrence of visual hallucination. How would one know that one's mind is hovering over one's body? Essentially, by seeming to see one's body at a distance, below. If or when one sees oneself in such a way, one might infer, on the one hand, that the mind has flown the coop and taken to the airways, or on the other hand, a more reasonable but less exciting notion, that one is hallucinating.

Which explanation is preferred will no doubt depend on one's philosophic preconceptions. The only real objection to the second one is that such hallucination might be thought impossible in normal (i.e., unintoxicated, nonpsychotic) people, except in their dreams. For that reason I have emphasized how extreme the effects of monotony can be, and now add that there may be similar effects in old age, what with the dulling of the senses and—often enough—a life devoid of excitement. At any rate, some of the nonpsychotic aged do have hallucinations (Bartlett, 1951), although most of them must be wise enough not to admit it to a doctor or to their relatives.

Even so, such experiences are rare, relatively speaking, and, occurring in later life, these cannot be the origin of one's ideas about the nature of one's self, though they may be cited in support. Much more fundamental in this respect are the situations and experience of everday life. The next step is to look at the evidence these situations provide, and the inferences one can, or must, make to the existence of a mind within and to its activities.

PRIMARY KNOWLEDGE OF MIND

One of C.S. Peirce's great insights was that one's knowledge of one's sensations, emotions or volitions "arises in connection with a judgment about external phenomena" (Goudge, 1960, p. 232), although his discovery seems not to have been appreciated by anyone. The "external" phenomena must be considered to include sensations from within the body (external to the mind) and the (illusory) external phenomena of which one is aware in imagery. The existence of hunger as a mental state may be known from stomach sensations, or because food smells very good: There is an element of learning involved here, and thus a genuine inference to a special motivational state. Fear may be known from both increased heart rate and imagery of possible future events. My stagefright I now recognize, as a result of learning, from a disturbed appetite and unwonted restlessness some hours before a lecture. Volitions and intentions are a more complex case, partly because we do not yet understand the initiation of motor action, whose control is more complex than we have assumed in the past (Vanderwolf, 1976). It is worth noting that one's own knowledge of one's intention is at times defective, when one finds oneself acting while still thinking about the possibility of doing so—or even, on occasion, while deciding not to (sometimes the basis on which indiscreet remarks are made). However, one's knowledge of intention, such as it is, may originate partly in a knowledge of how one has acted in like situations in the past, partly from somesthetic imagery of impending movement (or auditory imagery of what one is about to say), and partly from imagery of the situation resulting from this action or that.

Peirce's "judgment about external phenomena" appears to have a dual basis. What is external and what internal is judged by certain apparent conflicts of appearances *and* by a peculiar relation of external phenomena, so judged, to the phenomenal self (that is, one's body as perceived).

An immediate example of the inference based on conflict is the afterimage of a bright light that was discussed earlier. The visual evidence as one looks at a blank wall indicates the presence of a dark spot—but a spot that was not there before, that disappears after some seconds, that moves as the eyes move and is also visible briefly when the eyes are closed, and that others with good vision do not report seeing. The extensive conflict with past experience of marks on walls makes inevitable that inference that the spot is not real—not an external existent—but instead indicates the existence of something briefly active within oneself. My present deafness is similar in diagnosis. What I observe, the fact on which I can operate, is that others' speech is less intelligible. It naturally seems that they have changed: People mumble nowadays. But I also observe that others in the room seem to hear the jokes quite well, a conflicting fact that makes me reconsider my first conclusion: Instead of others' all having changed their speech habits, something has changed within me—but something not observable in itself, something to be discovered from that conflict of evidence.

Illusions illustrate another form of conflict. Being told that the cylinders of Figure 3 are all of the same size, I lay a ruler beside each one in succession and get a result requiring the conclusion either that the ruler changes as I move it from one to the next, or that the three are the same despite appearance and that this is a situation in which my visual system is aberrant.

Now to consider also the perceived relation of the world to one's own body. Here is the most fundamental basis of the inference to mind, the most obvious and the least discussed. The student will discover what I am talking about if, in a noisy room, he will put his hands over his ears and observe the change that results; or if he will go to the window, look out, and then close his eyes. As he closes his eyes a whole pattern of existence ceases, and returns as the eyes open again. While the eyes are closed he may still have imagery, he will undoubtedly be certain that the street or landscape still exists, but that is not the same thing. Such knowledge is a pallid alternative to the vividness that is contingent on having the eyes open. Without touching one's chair one can imagine the feeling of hardness and rigidity as the arm of the chair is gripped, but that is nothing to what one perceives when the hand is seen making actual contact with the wood. The brightness of the landscape, the liveliness of the conversation, the hardness of the chair, have a unique relation to the phenomena of the body: The eyes must be open, the ears must be uncovered, the hand must be in a certain place. The fundamental basis of inference to the

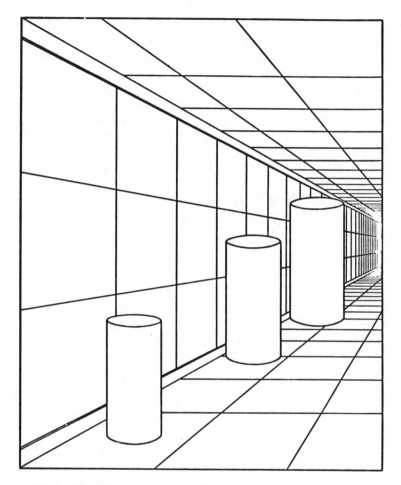

FIG. 3.   Visual illusion (the three cylinders are the same size). (From J. J. Gibson, 1950.)

existence of a mind within is the peculiar relation of some things to other things, the latter being parts of the body which as a result are known as sense organs. There is a close correlation in time, that is, between certain *existences*—things that simply *are*—and other existences. To call them visual or tactual or auditory or even, more generally, sensory, would beg the question: for what we are asking is, "What is the evidence from which I conclude that there is somewhere about this body a mind?" and "sensory," with its reference to an avenue leading to something internal, contains within itself the implication of the mind's existence.

In these circumlocutions I am trying to identify what is phenomenal with a minimum of inference, and to identify those relations between "external phenomena" that compel the adult to recognize the existence of the mind—however conceived of—and inevitably lead the growing infant to the same idea as his thought develops. And the same relations as he grows still more sophisticated tell him, fitfully and in part, what is going on within his mind. When he becomes very sophisticated indeed and begins to reflect on his thought and to be introspective—using these words as they are commonly used—he is apt to be surprised at times by what he discovers and what he fails to discover: "I don't know what got into me" to do so and so, "I can't imagine how I could have thought" such and such, or "The idea just came to me...." More on this when we come to the problem of creativity. Whether the activities of that strange—unknown, peculiar—entity within surprise the owner or not, his knowledge of its existence and its activities is inferential, from the phenomena of the outside world, including the behavior of his body and the illusory observations that are the result of imagery.

3

Biological Threads in the Philosophic Fabric

In this chapter I will try to show that ideas about the nervous system have been a major influence on both psychological and philosophic thought, with distorting effects even for those who deny any interest in neurology. If an influence of this kind exists, it should be recognized, to keep it under control. Subjective idealism is the prime example, but we also look from this biological point of view at other classical formulations, and conclude by asking how ideas about the brain, and "reductionism," may be used with a clarifying instead of a restricting and distorting effect.

The pervasive influence of neurological ideas in psychology may mean an unavoidable contamination of philosophy. In the theory of knowledge the two disciplines come together, and Descartes' great contributions to philosophy were after all presented in the context of a theory of behavior—which in turn was a theory of how the nervous system works, so "contamination" began early. Descartes' was truly a theory of behavior since it gave an account of how the mind controls the body's movements and how it gets the sensory information needed to do the controlling. Though the resulting picture of the nervous system as an input-output system only was grossly incomplete, this was a brilliant performance and so effective that the theory lasted almost into the present century, with changes in detail but little in principle; better ideas were obtained of how a nerve pathway transmits energy, for example, and better knowledge of the course taken by each pathway to and from the cortex, but there was still a very Cartesian concentration on sensory input to the cortex and an apparently independent motor output from it—independent, that is, in physiological terms. Linkage was a nonphysiological mental function. The first modification in principle

31

was made by Edward Lee Thorndike in 1898, and by Ivan Petrovich Pavlov independently in 1902. This we will return to shortly.

The effects of the Cartesian scheme are still evident in psychology. In philosophy, major lines of thought appear to have been attempts to live with or to escape the implications without renouncing the scheme itself. Parallelism for example escapes the anomaly of an interaction between substances totally unrelated—mind and matter—by endowing the material brain with all the powers of mind: a ridiculous solution. Philosophic idealism and the solipsism that Berkeley escaped by the skin of his teeth (in an appeal to divine intervention) are incompletely worked out Cartesian products; they can be shown to be either internally contradictory or, followed to the logical conclusion, wholly meaningless.

NEUROLOGICAL IDEAS IN PSYCHOLOGY

Until 1930 or thereabouts psychology was frankly neurological in an innocent sort of way; William James for example talked about habits as pathways worn in the brain, Wilhelm Wundt called his a physiological psychology. With Thorndike and Pavlov, the latter phrase took on real meaning, and a class of learning theory developed that permitted attack on a much wider range of phenomena than had ever been dealt with before, and began to show the real dimensions of the psychological problem. Unfortunately, these theories still had an essential lack, and Karl S. Lashley in a brilliant series of experiments between 1920 and 1930 showed that their neurological assumptions had little connection with the real world. Mostly I think because of Lashley's work, psychologists stopped casting their theoretical explanations in neurological terms but—the point I make here—this did not mean the end of the neurological influence. One's thinking may be constricted by ideas whose source one does not recognize and which one might reject if one did.

Figure 4 is a diagram of what is implied by the Cartesian theory of behavior as it was held, say, in the early nineteenth century. Incoming information to the brain from the sense organs is delivered to the "sensorium,"[5] a sort of

---

[5]At first, apparently the sensorium was the whole brain but was later restricted, as the following quotations show. Sir Charles Bell is given credit for showing in 1811 that the motorium has a separate locus (what he actually found was that motor nerves are separate from sensory nerves).

"Sir Isaac Newton and Dr. Samuel Clarke uniformly speak of the images of material things as being in that part of the brain called the *sensorium,* and perceived by the mind there present." Thomas Reid, 1803.

"The motorium is the portion of the nervous system through which self sends messages to the outer world." J. M. Baldwin, 1888.

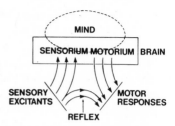

FIG. 4. Diagramming the relation of mind to brain in the Cartesian nervous system after Bell's separation of sensorium and motorium. An immaterial mind had a necessary role in any cognitive response, as the link between input and output. This did not apply to reflexes, which have their own built-in cross-connections.

bulletin board to be read by the mind, which may then initiate response via the "motorium." In this scheme, an immaterial mind plays a necessary part in adjustment to the environment (apart from the automatic, noncognitive reflex responses, controlled at lower levels in the nervous system). The fundamental modification by Thorndike, Pavlov, and later Watson, is represented in Figure 5, showing a direct sensorimotor cross-connection formed in the course of learning, so that sensory stimulation can elicit the new response directly. James and others of course had ideas of such cross-connections in learning, but apparently always in conjunction with a guiding mental process. For example, Lloyd Morgan thought that where there is learning there must be consciousness (which would extend consciousness through almost the entire animal world) for, he said, the learner must recall the pleasure of preceding rewards or the pain of preceding punishments to account for a change of response with experience. Thorndike was radical; he said there was no need to invoke any mental process to explain a cat's learning, and proposed instead that a "satisfying state of affairs" following response might act directly on the cat's brain to strengthen (i.e., by synaptic change) whatever pathway was active in producing that response, after it had occurred by chance; conversely when response is followed by an unsatisfactory or painful state of affairs. This opened a new era in psychology and determined the main lines of theoretical debate in the next 50 years or so. By that time it was clear that although Thorndike was wrong in major respects—cats demonstrably have intelligence, and there is more to learning than his "law of effect"—he was asking the right questions.

Looking again at Figure 5 (and at Figure 10, p. 84), one may see that no provision was made in this scheme for any independent activity by the brain; it proposed that the special function of the cortex is to make new connections possible but that all connections are ones that go straight through. At any given stage in learning, what the brain does is completely controlled by the

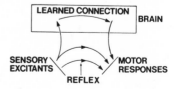

FIG. 5. The Cartesian nervous system, but with mind removed and transcortical connections substituted therefor.

sensory input. The brain itself initiates nothing (spontaneous firing by the neuron was not known), and no sensory message can be reworked or held for delivery to the muscles at a more appropriate time. Also, no connection between two incoming messages is possible: That is, all connections are S-R (stimulus-response), none S-S (stimulus-stimulus or sensory-sensory), which means that two sensations happening together cannot be associated; each may be associated with the same *response,* which is a different matter.

The denial of S-S associations nicely demonstrates the neurological influence. It was early discovered and emphasized in physiology that the neuron is polarized and conducts only in one direction. Hence two neurons parallel to one another at the same level in transmission cannot become connected—that is, cannot become able to excite one another—because the sending end of one cell (the axon) cannot excite the sending end of the second cell, as shown in Figure 6. Thus if cell *A* in the figure is excited by one sensory event, *B* excited by another, simultaneous, event, the two cortical processes cannot become connected (though they may be conditioned to both excite the same motor response). Exciting one cannot excite the other—though behavioral evidence clearly shows that this is wrong, as we will see (p. 87).

All this is still very Cartesian in denying that the nervous stystem by itself has any capacity for the essential creativity of thought. It was also consistent with—indeed, required by—neurophysiology of the early 20th century (the great change was made later by Adrian on spontaneous firing, in 1934, and Lorente de Nó on holding, in 1938). In 1920 the cerebral cortex was solely a variable transmitter: in the common analogy, a mere switchboard. Watson had full scientific warrant for denying any purely internal activity such as ideas or imagery, set or delayed response (in which excitation is held for short periods), or perception in the form of an elaboration of sensory input.

It is understandable that a psychologist might maintain such views, courageously, when well-established neurological conceptions leave him no alternative; but how can they be held after one has renounced all concern with

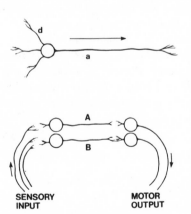

FIG. 6. *Above,* diagram of the neuron: *a,* axon; *d,* dendrites. The receiving end of the neuron is the dendrites; the axon sends but does not receive. *Below,* two neurons, *A* and *B,* receive sensory stimulation and excite motor output; being at the same level in sensorimotor transmission, they cannot excite one another, lying axon to axon instead of axon to dendrite. This is the conceptual nervous system of the physiologist in 1920: transmission is all prograde, not lateral or retrograde. For a crucial change, see Figures 11 and 12.

SENSORY INPUT

MOTOR OUTPUT

the nervous system in one's theorizing? It seems however that Watson's ideas, fused with Pavlov's, took on a life of their own, idependent of their source. In 1920, it was *unscientific* for the Behaviorist to talk about images or set or the association of ideas, and when in the 30's the "learning theorist" or neo-Behaviorist had given up cortical connections as a basis of theory it was *still* unscientific.

Today it is apparent that the nervous system is fully capable of handling ideation and creative thought. No one any longer attempts to explain such things away as Watson felt obliged to do, but there is a hard core of learning theorists who, denying any interest in neural function, still conspicuously limit their research and discussion to those features of behavior that Watson's neurophysiology could comprehend. Other psychologists, many of them, are set in a different theoretical posture—but still one that was determined by the long battle against Watsonian theory. They too may deny any interest in neurology—and still be deeply influenced by an earlier set of neurological ideas.

DESCARTES AND THE IMPRISONED KNOWER

In view of all this it is not entirely inconceivable that a philosopher today might hold to a theory of knowledge largely determined by an out-to-date, and quite erroneous, conception of the nervous system. Descartes did not originate the neurologizing—the brain was already regarded as the "seat" or "organ" of mind, and Augustine for example had wondered that the soul should know so little of the brain, to which it was closest, compared to other things farther removed—but Descartes achieved a new sophistication with his theory of how the nerves worked. (He accounted even for the phantom limb, a remarkable insight.) Their mechanical twitches and minute hydraulic pressures, as means of neural transmission, would reinforce existing ideas of the mind as essentially different from bodily functions, but the theory had a further and most important implication. Between mind and external reality was now interposed a crude communications system that in effect shut the mind off from the external world, which could be known only at secondhand. The consequence was that theory from Locke to Titchener—200 years—was concerned almost entirely with the sensory rather than the motor problem and, more fundamentally, with the plight of a mind imprisoned in the skull and informed only by a low-grade signaling system.[6] A parallel in today's terms: a prisoner shut in a dungeon with five TV screens—the five senses—

---

[6]Ogden (1951): the "slogan of despair" of the idealist in 1900 was "Ich kann nicht über mein eigenes Bewusstsein hinaus" (I can't escape from my own awareness); and Mountcastle (1975): "Each of us lives within the universe—the prison—of his own brain."

that picture a lively intricate world outside, but one that the prisoner has never been directly in contact with. How can he know whether the programs are live, or merely taped: how can he be sure there *is* any world such as that that appears on TV screens?

It was George Berkeley in 1710 who considered the predicament in which Descartes had left the soul and drew the conclusion that there is no reason to suppose that an outside world exists—at least, it is a matter of inference, theory rather than fact. It was a dazzling intellectual performance by a 24-year-old: dazzling to those who followed, so that they failed to see that the argument contained within it the seeds of its own destruction; and dazzling presumably to the author himself. It is understandable that a young man finding himself the possessor of an idea that appears to turn metaphysical philosophy inside out may not be impelled to search for fundamental flaws, especially if those whom his conclusions outrage are unable to refute them.

The argument opened the door to solipsism, the theory that only the thinker exists and the external world is a set of ideas within the thinker's own mind. In less extreme form, it appears in the question, whether there is any sound when a bell rings in the desert if there is no one there to hear it. It is the idea parodied by Lewis Carroll, when Tweedledum warns Alice that she was only something in the Red King's dream and if he awoke she would go out—bang!—just like a candle. Solipsism has been said at times to be logically inescapable, though obviously absurd. It has thus been an embarrassment to philosophy. But it is not inescapable, and nothing could illustrate more forcibly the hidden presence of neurological assumptions underlying philosophic thought: For solipsism, and related forms of idealism, are products of a particular conception of the nervous system, as merely a transmitter of information inward and of motor instructions outward. It is this conception that makes *knowing* a relation of mind to brain instead of a relation, primarily, of the whole organism to its environment. Abandon that Cartesian-Berkeleyan idea, and any logical necessity for solipsism disappears.

However, much more interesting is what happens if we do accept Berkeley's argument but follow it to its conclusion. The result is that it ends up in contradiction or, when contradiction is avoided, becomes meaningless.

For the moment then let us accept the conception of a mind that knows only its own sensory content, not any external object or even. We have seen what reason there is to doubt that there is such a state of affairs (p. 17), but let us look at the consequences of supposing it to be so. We then have a mind that knows itself and its content. No outside world is known to exist, though it may be guessed at, and we now consider the proposition that all apparent information from outside is illusory. The green of the grass, the hard chair on which I sit, the other persons in the room, all exist as ideas only.

But—ideas where? Not in a mind that is resident in this physical body that I call mine, for that body is itself only an idea. This is the point at which the argument leaves the rails in the implicit retention of the physical identity of the solpsistic thinker. The whole case depends on the idea that sensory information corresponds to no external existence, and the thinker's body must be illusion as much as any part of the universe depicted on the thinker's sensorium (on the TV screens of the imprisoned knower, in the analogy proposed above). Otherwise, contradiction.

That contradiction, dimly realized, is what makes for absurdity: for solipsism otherwise loses meaning instead of being absurd. Solipsism is self-contradictory, and thus absurd, when it is taken to mean that this chair and room and other persons in the room exist as ideas within the head of this sensorily known observer, myself, for the observer as a physical person does not exist either. Popper (1972, p. 38) has said that the theory that the world "is just my dream" cannot be refuted though it is obviously false; but all he considers is a form of Samuel Johnson's refutation, which of course was no refutation at all (Sam kicked a stone, to show that it was really real). But the theory is readily refuted by pointing out to the "dreamer" that he is a puppet in the dream too, so the dream cannot be his. The world, and all physical existence, may indeed be a dream, but not the dream of any human thinker.

Now let us try the argument without the contradiction. The mind of the solipsist comprises all existence, and thus cannot itself be comprised by anything else. Also, it cannot be a function of or dependent on an individual human body, the solipsist's. It is instead coextensive with the physical universe, and in effect *is* the universe. Within that universe no distinction of mind from matter is possible—all is mental. Yet that latter statement has little meaning, for in this context the significance of "mental" lies in a contrast with "physical" and that contrast is no longer possible. Any feeling that this conceptual product of the original argument is an *idealism* as distinct from materialism is merely a hangover, an emotional residual, a preference for one word rather than another as a result of a formerly held but—according to the theory—erroneous distinction. One can only say that the upshot of all this intricate argument is that one ends up in a monism instead of dualism; otherwise, no change.

For we are back where we started. The original problem has reappeared, in the question of how to deal theoretically with the thought and behavior of the (ideal) men and women in relation to their (ideal) environments, and even how to understand the behavior of the (ideal) physical self. In other words, the mind-body problem has reappeared, with the sole change that one may if one wishes consider both mind and body of one of these individuals to be items in an all-encompassing mind, thus constituting a monism—and clearly, opening the door to the identity theory of the relation of mind to body. What difference then remains between such idealism and the equally extreme theory of materialism? In each case, denial of an opposed mode of existence robs the identifying adjective ("ideal" or "material") of its meaning in this context, and we are left with a monism. No qualification: monism is monism, and "materialism," for those who dislike the word, can mean that matter and mind both are ideas in the mind of God, if there is a God.

It is unlikely that anyone ever took solipsism seriously, except as an embarrassment. But it still has modern echoes (e.g., Huxley, 1962; Mountcastle, 1975) that are encountered every now and then, the writer taking the Cartesian neurology for granted in the assumption that what one can know is one's sensations. This can lead to some surprising conclusions.

Two earlier examples will make the point. The first is the conclusion of Ernst Mach that psychology and physics have the same subject-matter. As an eminent physicist (his name preserved in "Mach-1," "Mach-2," etc., with respect to air speeds) he might be thought to know what he was talking about. How could he come to such a conclusion? But consider the thinker bottled up in his own field of consciousness, with the problem of decoding the signals presented on the sensorium. *Those signals* are what the thinker deals with; whether they originate with human beings or with the hardware of physics, the scientific material is the same. An absurd conclusion, but arising from the same source as solipsism.

The second example is Bertrand Russell, also eminent, in philosophy as well as in mathematics. In his book *Philosophy,* Russell affirms that Watson could not see one of his rats in the maze, nor a physiologist see a living brain: for direct observation of an external object is not possible, and what one sees is in one's own brain (the sensorium?). The nature of external events "can only be inferred by the help of physics." Russell freely states that any other conclusion would be preposterous, for "the event which constitutes seeing comes at the end of a series of events" that begins with the object that one seems to see. This stands the truth on its head, for almost any other conclusion would be more sensible than Russell's. The argument is self-consuming; he takes for granted the physicist's results in order to cast doubt on what the physiologist sees, but if the latter can discover things in the outside world only with the aid of physics, where did physics get the aid necessary to make its own observations in the first place? The conclusion is silly, hardly worth disputing except to show, once more, how distorting the effects of an underlying neurological assumption can be. Any suggestion by an idealist that makes doubtful the direct knowledge of an external reality is nonsense, for it ultimately derives from taking for granted the physical existence of our sensory equipment, thought of as intervening between the knower and the all physical existence; which is a contradiction.

PARALLELISM, EPIPHENOMENALISM, INTERACTIONISM

It thus appears that the argument of subjective idealism leads to a monism which differs from materialism only as a form of words. If one feels better by thinking of all existence as ideal, items in the mind of God or in some other all-encompassing mind, well and good, but that view hardly permits any further belief that mind and body are not of the same kind of stuff. Quite the contrary. For the biological scientist, neither theory nor experiment is affected by adopting such harmless philosophic views.

Much the same thing may be said of parallelism, epiphenomenalism, and one form at least of interactionism: the one that regards mental processes as lawful, so that mind and body, though unlike, may operate together as a deterministic system.

Parallelism is the theory that mental events and brain events run side by side, perfectly correlated but not causally related: in the old analogy, like two clocks that stay perfectly in step but not because either influences the other. It has been highly regarded as a way of avoiding commitment to an interaction of mind and body—or even worse, identifying them—while recognizing how closely they are related. But this is evasion rather than avoidance, for it is an empty solution. It maintains the separation between mind and body only by allowing the brain to have all the powers of the mind. It makes Shakespeare's mind something entirely different from his body—but it seems to be overlooked that it was his body, his brain and peripheral nerves and hand, that wrote the plays. Parallelism says that the actors in the theatre, representing anger and fear and love in Shakespeare's plays, did so with no guidance from their conscious minds; whatever thought there may have been in those entirely separate minds, the *bodies* functioned on the stage as self-programmed robots. To account for the writing of Newton's *Principia,* the movements of the hand and fingers that produced the manuscript without guidance from Newton's thought, one must suppose that his brain had equivalent skills.

Apart from the evident absurdity, a more general question is raised. What meaning, what real significance, is there in saying that brain and mind, as conceived of in this way, are separate? Similarly, epiphenomenalism also regards human awareness as entirely distinct from the brain, but only as a kind of by-product of its activity—a kibitzer that does not affect the play of the cards. The brain must have all the powers of human thought without being itself conscious: Here again, what can it mean to think of such a mind as distinct from the brain's cognitive activities? A brain that functions in every respect like a mind *is* a mind; are there then two minds here? In the famous two-clock comparison with parallelism, the two clocks are separate entities by virtue of their separation in space; if in addition to being identical in function they also occupied the same space, as mental activity and brain activity appear to do (visual perception, auditory perception, verbal fluency, verbal comprehension, and so on each relating to particular parts of the brain), they would be one clock. To paraphrase C.S. Peirce's principle of pragmatism: Consider what practical effects such a distinction of mind from brain may have; then our conception of those effects is the whole conception of the distinction. The practical effects are null, the distinction is merely verbal.

A closely related argument applies to what I referred to earlier as a lawful interactionism. Here the mind acts on and is acted on by the brain according to rules that it is the business of psychological research to discover. If as we saw in Chapter 2 the activity of mind is not known directly—if I know the minds of others by inference from their behavior, and know my own mind from judgements based on external phenomena—then the situation is this: The objective evidence tells me—the dualist—that something complex goes on inside my head; part of this I know is the activity of sensory and motor nerves and the brain, but part of it—I believe—must have a delicacy and complexity that no nervous system is capable of; I conclude therefore that *something else* is active also. It is perfectly evident that the conclusion is hasty, at a time when the limits of delicacy and complexity of brain function are not yet known, but the more general question again is this: Supposing it exists, what are the criteria by which the *something else* is classed as nonphysical? It is known from its effects only, and even if its nature is mysterious it is no more mysterious than magnetism or gravity or other things that the physicist knows only by their effects. In any other field of thought, what has lawful physical effects is regarded as part of the physical universe; on what basis is another conclusion justified here—apart from unthinking preconception?

This whole question has been re-opened by the "split-brain" patients of Bogen (1969), Gazzaniga (1970), and Sperry (1968, 1970). In these patients the left and right hemispheres of the brain were disconnected surgically for the relief of otherwise intractable epilepsy. After operation the activity of the two hemispheres could be very different and a patient might seem to have two minds, a left-hand and a right-hand mind. Sensory and motor connections in the nervous system are crossed, so the right hemisphere gets its information about the outside world from the left side of the body (and the left half of the visual field), while the left gets its information from the right side. In these patients, as in the majority of the population, the language centers were on the left side, so the left hemisphere could talk to the experimenters but the right could let them know what was going on, internally, only through its control of the left hand. (The right hemisphere does however have a low-level comprehension of speech and of printed language.) In these circumstances one hemisphere can be given information the other lacks, by projecting it to one side while the patient fixates the center of the projection screen; or the two hemispheres can be given different instructions and carry out their different tasks at the same time—among a group of objects out of sight, for example, the left hand searches for and finds one object, the right hand a different object.

So—two minds in one head? It would be embarrassing for the dualist if he must conclude that an immaterial mind can be cut in two by the surgeon's scalpel. Sperry (1970) has dealt with the situation by proposing that the mind is a continuously emergent product of the brain's activity, emphasizing both the separateness and the inseparability of "mental forces" and "physiological forces" as they interact. For example:

> the subjective phenomena of conscious experience are conceived to be direct emergent properties of brain excitation, inseparable from the brain process and its structural constraints, but nevertheless different from and more than the sum of the electrochemical and physiological activities (p. 136).

This is not epiphenomenalism, though it may sound like it, for the mental processes have a physiological action ("consciousness does things"). The emergent idea is a slippery one, its meaning hard to pin down precisely, but here it allows Sperry to recognize the presence of two minds in the split-brain patient without having to suppose that the mind can be chopped up as a brain can be.

Sir John Eccles has taken a different tack, based on a more classical approach to dualism. Originally (Eccles, 1953) he minimized the conflict of interactionism with the law of conservation of energy by arguing that very little energy would be expended by the will and the conscious mind if they acted on the brain by influencing it at the level of subatomic particles and only within the range of the uncertainty principle. More recently (Eccles, 1973) he has adopted Sir Karl Popper's indeterminism and therefore can view small violations of the conservation laws with equanimity. He can then deal specifically with the split-brain problem simply by denying the existence of the second mind on the right side. In Popper and Eccles (1977) he concedes that the right hemisphere continues to carry out complex functions, but since it cannot talk it gives no evidence of consciousness and so does not have a mind.

But is that a test of consciousness? What are the signs of consciousness in the year-old baby, in the deaf-mute, or for that matter in the porpoise and the chimpanzee? The activity of the disconnected right hemisphere includes memory, perception, and purpose. It lacks speech, but by way of compensation it has better pattern perception than the left hemisphere—better recognition of faces, for example. It is capable of feelings of propriety. A young woman patient was shown a picture of a nude, presented in the left visual field for perception by the right hemisphere. She blushed and showed embarrassment, but could not say why. It seems obvious that the embarrassment was a right-hemisphere event, which adds to the evidence of consciousness on the right side of the brain. To avoid that conclusion, Eccles argues that the visual information must somehow have reached the left hemisphere, via uncut pathways at the base of the brain. It seems likely that this might happen where intensity is concerned, but all the clinical evidence is opposed to the idea that it could occur with visual pattern, and in any case it is difficult to accept the idea that the left hemisphere was embarrassed by the presence of an object it could not recognize.

All such difficulty is avoided by Sperry's emergentism, but here again we must ask: What meaning is there in saying that the emergent consciousness is not simply an aspect or property of the physical brain and its activity, as magnetism is a physical property of moving electrons? By what criteria is it distinguished from the more molar aspects of that activity? What specific properties has it that mean it is not part of the physical universe? Until that question is answered, with respect to Eccles' formulation as well as Sperry's, the separateness of mind and brain is verbal only and can have no empirical significance.

NEUROLOGIZING: USEFUL TOOL BUT HANDLE WITH CARE

Let us now consider the proper use of neurological ideas, and the meaning of "reductionism." This is a topic on which misunderstanding is easy, and it may be vain for me to hope that misunderstanding can be avoided here—but one must try.

Properly done, relating psychological things to neurological things—the mental to the anatomical and physiological—has value both as stimulant and as corrective. It has a bad name with philosophers and psychologists (but not all of them), due in the first place to having often been done badly (and dogmatically), and in the second place to being not understood when done right. Properly done, reductionism does not substitute neurophysiology for psychology; when it assumes that pain or ecstasy consists of neural firing it recognizes the reality of pain and joy at the same time; it does not try to explain them away. It is the method of theoretical analysis followed resynthesis, whose validity depends strictly on whether the result accords with the psychological as well as the neurological evidence. However, its value is that it may do this by showing the need of re-examining one or other of the two bodies of evidence and the conclusions drawn from it. Really, it can destroy nothing but error, by psychologist *or* neurophysiologist, and its positive effect may be to show an experimenter where to look for new evidence or a theorist how to look at the available evidence from another aspect.

A different failure of understanding is to suppose that identifying mental processes with physiological processes is mere translation, done only to sound scientific and impressive. A critic reviewing a book of mine said that "a connection between cell-assemblies" is no improvement on "an association of ideas," if ideas are cell-assemblies. But there are constraints on the functioning of cell-assemblies; if the identification is right, these constraints affect the theory of ideas. For example, it becomes necessary to conclude that what one usually thinks of as an idea must be a complex of simpler ideas (i.e., a constellation of cell-assemblies). One can readily see in that case how the idea of the self, as complex, may consist in part of the same components as the idea of another (p. 24). It also suggests a mechanism of Freudian symbolism, if the idea of a church steeple and the idea of an erect penis are complexes that share a common core (a sub-idea of verticality); it relates to James' notion that the same idea can never recur in thought—an overstatement apparently, but cell-assembly theory does suggest strongly that the "same idea" occurring in different contexts may have the same core but differ in fringe components; and so on. The identification of "idea" with "cell-assembly" or "complex of assemblies" is not vacuous but affects theory. Ideas have developed new properties.

The stimulus of reduction can be in either direction. Our concern here is its value for the development of psychological concepts, but I note in passing that there is no superiority of one source of evidence over the other. Psychological facts can show the need of revision of neurological theory. A clear example is Hunter's delayed-response experiments, which showed that there was error in the current conception of brain function which Watson accepted (p. 9). What Hunter was saying, and Watson might have said, was that the neurophysiologists were wrong. Unfortunately—for them as well as for psychology—neurophysiologists of the day did not give much weight to the behavioral evidence, and the indicated revision of physiological theory had to wait.

What has given reductionism a bad name is the conclusion, after a theoretical analysis of a mental variable has been made and it is "reduced" to some pattern of neural activity, that the mental process in effect no longer exists. This is the nothing-but fallacy: Mental activity is a myth, what *really* exists is something in the brain. Such an attitude is absurd, but in certain circumstances it seems easy to accept. I once listened to a debate between a hard-boiled physiologist and a clinical psychologist who was evidently less hard-boiled, since he did not defend himself well. The question concerned anxiety and how it should be treated. Said the physiologist, "Either you think anxiety is something in the soul, which is superstition, not science, or you must agree that something has gone wrong in the patient's brain—so it is the brain you have to treat, not the mind." What he meant was, stop the psychotherapy and find out what drug to give. This is the nothing-but fallacy: If anxiety and thought and memory are identified with neural activities, it may be said that there is nothing there but those neural activities; anxiety and thought and memory have been replaced as impalpable and unreal, illusory.

But this *is* fallacy. It is comparable to concluding, in physical science, that sunshine is a myth, all that really exists is a bombardment of photons; or that the desk at which I sit is illusion, the reality being only a complex of molecules—or indeed, that the reader of this passage also is illusion and mirage. Obviously this is all nonsense; when a complex is reduced, theoretically, to its component parts, the whole still exists. Anxiety must be a pattern of firing of neurons in the limbic system, but the pattern is as real as the individual neurons.

For all this there is a clarifying analogy that allows us to see that there *is* a limited sense in which the thing analyzed, the whole, does not exist—but only at another level of analysis. At its own level it is still there, as shown in the following.

An engineer designing a bridge must think at several levels of complexity. His conception of the bridge as a whole is very molar, in terms let us say of a center span, two side spans, two piers, and two abutments. Now when he turns to the design of the center span he begins to think in terms of lower-order units such as steel beams, rivets or welding, and masses of reinforced concrete. However, these items are still very molar. Any engineer if asked would say that a steel I-beam is just a special arrangement of atoms or of electrons, neutrons, and so forth. At this last level of analysis a bridge *is nothing but* a complex constellation of atoms, and at this level of analysis a steel I-beam is merely a convenient fiction, a crude concession to the limitations of human thought which would be incapable of planning in more microscopic terms. *At this level of analysis* there is indeed nothing but atoms or atomic particles. But there are other levels of analysis; from the point of view of a practical man, all this stuff about atoms may be fine in theory (and may even be useful when one thinks about improving the quality of steel) but when it comes to bridge-building it is no more than theory. At this level of analysis the I-beam is an elementary unit, obviously real and no fiction. Reality now is steel and concrete.

So from one point of view, reality is the atom, the steel beam being a convenient way of dealing with large numbers of atoms in a particular pattern; while from another, the steel that is heavy and cold and resistant to distortion is reality, and atoms are theoretical items only. For different modes of thought, different realities: "reality" referring evidently to the mode of being that one takes for granted as the starting point of thought.

Now the behavioral problem. At a certain level of theoretical analysis there is no reality but the firing of single neurons: emotions, intentions, and consciousness are convenient fictions. But human thought does not restrict itself to any one level of analysis when seeking explanations, and those conceptions (of emotions, intentions and consciousness) are, like that of a steel I-beam, necessary as well as convenient for other levels of analysis. They are fiction only at more microscopic level; when one is dealing with the phenomena of everyday experience and of the clinic, fear and anger and grief are only too real.

For scientific purposes also these conceptions or others like them will always be necessary. Even if we could identify the part played by every one of the 9 or 10 or more billion neurons in the brain, the human mind of the scientist is obviously incapable of thinking of the whole activity in such terms. It is not possible to follow the varying patterns of the firing of these cells as individual units. What one must identify is the larger patterns of the activity, and it is just such larger patterns that we know as anger or fear—or love, or mirth or pride. The wood is as real as the trees, a storm is as much a reality as the raindrops and gusts of wind of which it is composed.

Thus reductionism is not a means of abolishing psychological entities and processes but a way of learning more about them. In principle, the attempt to identify mental events with brain processes is an attempt to see them in a different context. Emotion as distinct from emotional behavior is a theoretical entity; when one looks for a physiological process to identify it with (again theoretically), one may find that one of its supposed properties cannot be included in the physiological translation—but that some other property, not thought of before, is suggested at once. The question then is whether the modified idea of what emotion is or how it takes place makes behavioral sense, as one returns to the actual observation of human behavior. With luck, the theoretical conception has been sharpened, and the agreement of theory with fact improved.

That is a very general statement: Let me make it more specific with an example. In my attempt some 30 years ago to develop a general theory of behavior, including a theory of thought, it was evident that some of the mystery might disappear if thought could be regarded as a series of activities in small groups of neurons in the brain ("cell-assemblies"). For example, attention and set, which were wholly without explanation at the time, would at once become intelligible; psychologists need no longer avoid such conceptions on the ground that there was something wrong about them since they lacked rational explanation. So far so good: clearly the theory being worked out would be useful—and although it was reductionistic, its immediate force was *not in the direction of getting rid of a mentalistic conception but just the opposite:* It restored one that had been lost because no one could see how it worked. A further effect however is of more interest here. The new theoretical conception was incompatible with widely accepted views of perception, including my own view. It suggested a quite different basis of perceived identity from what I had thought was established fact; but when I now looked at the experimental evidence again, from the point of view of the neurological conceptions I was trying out, it was plain that there were large gaps in the evidence. The new idea of perception was distasteful, to me, but not contrary to existing fact, and because of the explanatory power of the neurological conceptions in other areas I went ahead and published. Then a series of experimental studies supported this general line of thought, and most explicitly confirmed the new and originally distasteful theory of perception.

It is not suggested that reductionism always has such useful effects; I have much more often been wrong than right, and here describe a case in which I was lucky and reductionism paid off. My point is that attempting to identify the neural bases of psychological variables is a way of probing and testing and—with luck—improving one's perceptions of reality at the level of observable behavior.

4 The Evolution of Mind and Behavior

The argument of this chapter is that the behavioral signs of mind and consciousness are evident only in the mammals, with the possible exception of some of the larger-brained birds; that relatively small-brained mammals like the rat or the hamster may have very small minds (like the penguins of Anatole France's *Penguin Island,* to whom the Lord gave souls but of a smaller size)—but still minds, whereas fish and reptiles, and most birds, seem to be reflexively programmed and give little evidence of that inner control to which the term mind refers. The best evidence of continuity, in the development from lower to higher mammals, is to be found not in their intellectual attainments, their capacities for learning and solving problems, but in their motivations and emotions. Man is evidently the most intelligent animal but also, it seems, the most emotional.

THE NEURAL BASIS OF DEVELOPMENT

Our knowledge of the way the nervous system developed is obviously theoretical. Not only is the fossil record incomplete: At best it can only tell us about the size and shape of the brain, or the brain and spinal cord, and it is a long step from the size of the brain to knowing how it functioned. A bigger brain does not necessarily mean a higher level of performance. In practice, we must also assume that we can tell what the course of evolution was from some animals now living, as far as learning and intelligence are concerned. We may for example assume that among mammals the following represent behavioral levels like those through which our own ancestors progressed: rat, cat, dog, monkey, ape, man (I pick species for which there is extensive behavioral information). This is only an assumption, but it is more reasonable than one might suspect, because of the fact that the brains of all living vertebrates are built on the same master plan, and that the brains of mammals in particular (including those listed above) are identical except in size and the relative sizes of the component parts; they are extremely complex, and years would be needed before a student could become able to identify the internal structures of, say, the monkey brain and master what is known about their interrelations—but having done so, a week or two might be enough to find the same structures in the brain of another mammal; and as for the interrelations, he would know them already.

Now it seems evident that the nervous system must have evolved in the first place as a communications network, a role it still plays. With the emergence of thought in the mammalian brain, it has taken on a further role, but the primitive reflexive connection of receptors (sensory cells) with effectors (muscle and gland) is as vital for the mammal as for any other animal. It is no good for the eyes or nose of a hungry animal to be excited by food unless the word gets to the legs and the muscles of the jaws, so the food is reached and eaten; and every step the animal takes requires a coordination of muscles that is achieved by the nervous system. Breathing and blood supply are regulated by neural connections, and so with the processes of digestion. The nervous system of the higher animal is still a communications network, integrating the activities of the organism and harmonizing them with the normal environment by the transmission of sensory information.

G.H. Parker, from his studies of living animals, concluded that the first step toward a nervous system was a specialization of some cells for contraction— that is, as muscle cells—following a course represented in Figure 7. The development begins with cells in the outside wall. These contractile cells then migrate inward while others, still external, specialize in excitability and become elongated, to connect with the inner-lying muscle cells and excite them. A further stage is the appearance of interneurons entirely inside the organism that connect neuron with neuron or neuron with muscle; and finally, the massing of interneurons in the central nervous system, like the central switchboard of a telephone exchange. There is a long step from an early nerve-net organization of which *D,* Figure 7, might be a part, to the far more efficient operation of the central structure. As far as I can discover, the course of that later development in unknown, but it is evident that the development took place twice, independently, in vertebrates and invertebrates, for the two follow quite different plans. In the vertebrate the central nervous system forms a single mass of brain and spinal cord dorsal to the alimentary canal—that is, next the back, in the spinal column—but in the invertebrate is ventral and consists of a series of separate masses (ganglia) connected by relatively thin neural strands.

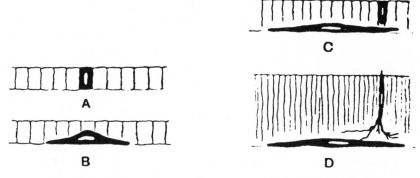

FIG. 7. Early developments leading to the nervous system. *A*, a cell in the outside wall of the animal is both excitable and contractile—acts as both sense organ and muscle. *B*, further specialization as muscle only, having migrated inward and now excited only by the outer cells. *C*, another cell has begun to specialize for excitability, as well as for transmission toward the motor cell. *D*, the primitive nerve-muscle combination. *B* represents the level of the sponge, *D* that of a more efficient coelenterate. From Parker (1911).

In considering the evolution of the vertebrate brain the first obvious point that is discussed is its size in different species: ranging from a small fraction of a gram to about 7000 grams. It is immediately evident that size alone does not determine the brain's level of function: does not, that is, determine intelligence. The elephant has a brain almost four times as large as man's (5000 as compared to 1300 grams), and if there is one thing certain in comparative psychology it is that the elephant is not four times as smart as a human being. Within the human species, again, brain weights of normally functioning individuals vary from about 1000 grams to about 2000, and the differences do not correlate with estimated level of intelligence; some persons with large brains have been very capable, like Samuel Johnson and Georges Cuvier (over 1800 gms), but others have been far less so, and some with small brains like Anatole France (about 1100 gms) have nonetheless had outstanding ability (von Bonin, 1963).

But size must still be important, and there have been persistent attempts to explain why the elephant, for example, or the bottle-nose porpoise, should have a larger brain than man. Such attempts assume that it takes a large brain to control a large body. The notion is apparently that only the excess of brain tissue, over and above what is necessary for that control, is available to provide a basis of intelligence. Thus one may calculate the ratio of brain weight to body weight to put the elephant in his place: his brain is only 1/600th of the total weight of the animal, whereas man's is about 1/45th of his weight. So we conclude that man has more brain to spare for thought and intelligence. But the fact is that the elephant, despite that very low ratio of brain to body weight, is a very intelligent animal, so there is something wrong with the argument; and worse, the mouse has as good a ratio as man and the squirrel monkey a much better one (1/12). The brain-weight: body-weight ratio has fascinated anthropologists and students of evolution, and various formulas have been devised to make it work better (Jerison, 1973). We need not go into these complicated schemes because they provide no rational basis for an index of intelligence, which is what they are meant to do. It may be that one of these can provide valid evidence that *Australopithecus* is a collateral ancestor of modern man, by showing that he was proportioned similarly, but it provides little evidence of the level of intelligence more than is provided by the relatively large brain—apart from the size of the body. It is true that a larger brain tends to function at a higher level, and it is also true that brain size and body size are correlated. This last fact however is not because it requires a big brain to manage a big body.

There are other reasons why the two should be related in size. A big body is needed to carry the skull that contains a big brain, and the female must be large enough to have a pelvis that permits delivery of the relatively large-brained infant at term. As for the neural control of a big body, heavily muscled, a thick spinal cord may be required and therefore a large motor cortex and cerebellum, though that is not a self-evident proposition. Twice as many muscle cells do not need twice as many neurons to control them unless there is also some element of increased agility or intricacy of movement. In that case we would be dealing with a brain that is larger because it is functioning at a higher level, and not merely with one that is big because the body is big.

The conformation of the brain is a different matter, as is the relative size of its different parts. In the example preceding, of motor skill, the presence of well-developed motor structures in the brain might be interpreted as having nothing to do with intellectual capacity; but a moment's thought reminds one of the dexterity required for making and using tools and weapons, which by common agreement must have been a main avenue of man's intellectual advance. One might then expect that a large motor cortex would be a requirement for reaching the level of *Homo sapiens*. The other main avenue, also agreed on, was language, and it is now clear that we must regard language as a highly developed motor skill, as well of course as a perceptual skill on the part of the listener (Kimura & Archibald, 1974).

On the perceptual side, the crucial question of intelligence and thought is the extent to which there is an autonomy of cerebral function: how far the brain is dominated by the present sensory input, how far it is capable of an internal activity that transcends the present situation. We will return to this point shortly; I raise it here to show the theoretical significance of the relation of the mass of association cortex to that of sensory cortex, which I have referred to as the A/S ratio. If sensory cortex is extensive and association cortex small, there is little prospect of the occurrence of any activity in the brain other than that determined by the present sensory environment. *Sensory cortex* here means the total mass of the several sensory projection areas; *association cortex* is the old name for the regions that are neither sensory nor motor, on the reasonable assumption that the association of sensory events must take place here, though of course other functions must be based here too. In particular, this must be the key to the thought process.[7] The essential character of thought involves imagery and other, high-order, representative activity, corresponding not to the present situation but to others of the past or the possible future. This cannot take place in sensory cortex, which is of course under the full control of the present sensory environment. Also, as above, if association cortex is small compared to sensory cortex it too will be dominated, and thus a small A/S ratio means a low level of thought and intelligence. A large A/S ratio does not guarantee intelligence, but it is a requirement (necessary but not sufficient).

This is not a very practical index, it is true. Even with existing mammals there are no quantitative values available for the extent of primary sensory cortex; with a good deal of work they could be obtained from serial sections of the brain, but there is no such possibility with a fossil brain. Nevertheless, it is interesting to find Holloway (1974) emphasizing the indications of a small visual area in the australopithecine brain compared to an enlarged parietal and temporal cortex that must have been mostly association cortex. From this and other indications Holloway concludes that the human brain was already distinctive, divergent from the main primate stem, as long as three million years ago.

Man's disproportionately large A/S ratio we may see as an essential factor in his intellectual development, but it can hardly be the whole story. We know also that something else occurred to make his brain distinctive, although it is not something that would be detectable in the fossil record: the lateralization of function, the specialization of left and right hemispheres for different roles, which is not known in any other species. Presumably this is an essential part of the whole development. But it seems clear that there is still something else, whose nature we do not know but which makes the human brain more efficient, gram for gram or kilogram for kilogram, than any other. Efficiency here means the capacity to process information and record it, to abstract from it and to generalize, and to perform the creative syntheses that so far outdo the analogous syntheses of other animals: all this as shown in human behavior. The size of the brain is evidently important, up to some threshold value

---

[7] It is important to remember that thought cannot be a solely cortical activity. The cortex is closely connected, throughout its extent, with subcortical structures that must be involved in any of its activities and it is better to think of the cortex as a vital component rather than as the seat of thought in itself.

perhaps of 1000 grams, after which some other variable is increasingly important. It is this variable that permits a relatively small brain like Anatole France's to make its owner an outstanding figure among his literary contemporaries, and lack of it that accounts for the fact that some much larger brains have been possessed by morons.

What can this other variable be? A first suggestion is likely to be that the human superiority is due to the possession of language, as a by-product of the lateralization of function in the human brain, but this does not account for the possession of language itself. As we will see later (p. 116), language, though an important adjunct, cannot be the main mover in thought. A possibility is some metabolic development in the human nervous system that makes the individual neuron more efficient, perhaps because of a better blood supply. This seems unlikely. A more likely theoretical possibility is found in the finer structure of the brain and the greater frequency of short-axon cells than in other species, on the assumption that a good proportion of these are inhibitory. In a large brain there must be a problem of "noise," the activity of neurons firing spontaneously, or continuing to fire with inappropriate timing. The effect on thought is returned to later (p. 114). Here I note that Rakic (1975) has drawn attention to the frequency of short-axon cells, or what the conference from which his report originated preferred to call local circuit neurons (LCNs), in the human brain. In posterior cortex these presumptively inhibitory neurons increase with phylogenesis: visual cortex, rabbit, 31% LCNs; cat, 35%; rhesus monkey, 45%; and man, about 75%. Rakic quotes Ramón y Cajal, that brilliant observer: "The functional superiority of the human brain is intimately linked up with the prodigious abundance... of the so-called *neurons with short axons*" (p. 301) and "intellectual power... [does] not depend on the size or number of cerebral neurons but on the richness of the connective processes...." (p. 304)—implying also that it does not depend on brain size except as this may make the richness possible.

As the mammalian forebrain increases in size there is also an increase of inhibitory LCNs, although presumably without a close correlation between the two variables; a large brain, with a relative lack of LCNs, may be outperformed by a smaller one with more LCNs. This may account not only for the human superiority to the elephant, but also for the low correlation between brain weight and intellectual performance within the human species.

THE EVIDENCE OF EXISTING BEHAVIOR

Now let us consider evidence from existing animals, whose brains can be examined directly and whose behavior can actually be seen. The evidence is more direct but we must keep in mind that it is only theoretically relevant to the course of evolution, since it depends on the assumption that the levels of behavioral complexity that we know correspond to the stages through which evolution passed, at least roughly.

First the question of where mind and consciousness appeared. Evolution is a continuous process; if consciousness is an attribute of the active human brain, this might be thought to mean that consciousness is present in some degree wherever there is neural activity. But this need not follow. I have already invoked the physicist's idea of a critical mass in arguing earlier that we need not attribute consciousness to computers. There are degrees and degrees of consciousness, but even the simplest or most primitive may have occurred in evolution only when a certain very large number of neurons made possible a certain pattern of complexity of neural firing. Thus there may be so to speak a quantitative continuity—a steadily increasing number of neurons— resulting in qualitative discontinuity. The existence of consciousness in the higher animal does not mean necessarily that it exists in some degree in lower ones.

I have already proposed that consciousness is a product or accompaniment or form of thought, and I now point out that no one attributes thought or consciousness to the body of a chicken with its head cut off, despite its activity for some seconds after the head is cut off, nor to the lower part of the spinal cord of a human paraplegic though it continues to serve its reflexive functions. Consciousness can hardly be identified from any simple motor index, for it is a variable state that can produce complete immobility, as in listening, or extreme activity as in running to catch a bus. It is not all-or-none, for it is present but impaired after taking in alcohol, or in one who can talk while recovering from a knockout but later remembers nothing of the conversation. It is qualitatively different in the vivid rememberable dream from what it is in crossword-puzzle solving, or in anger or in anxiety. A variable state, as thought patterns are variable.

But identification becomes possible if, as above, we assume that it is a function of the thought process. We lack evidence of thought, and thus of consciousness, in most birds as well as in fish, but this may well change with further work (it has not really been looked for, experimentally, except in mammals), and it may be that thought and consciousness are present but not to the extent characteristic of even the small-brained mammals with their prominent cortices (the cortex is rudimentary in birds). Also, in attributing consciousness to the mouse or the hamster, we need suppose that it is the fully developed consciousness of the large-brained mammals, including a conception of *self* and *other* that is implied by the occasional manifestations of altruism and empathy.

Thought in birds, if it exists, must be a sort of one-track process compared to thought in the mammal. The method of training a falcon is to capture an adult bird and then by close confinement in darkness, hand-feeding, and later feeding while the bird is still held by a sort of leash, convincing it that food is to be had only at the hand of the falconer, so that the falcon can then be turned loose to catch prey—other birds—and bring them to the falconer. Earlier learning, from the period when the falcon fed itself on its own prey, appears to be completely over-ridden by the later experience in a way that is quite impossible with a mammal. Consistent with this, while not in itself decisive evidence, is the readiness with which even as clever a bird as the crow can be imprinted on a human being, taken early from the nest and looked after by man; the crow thereafter avoids other crows and consorts with its keeper. Something of the sort is possible with some mammals such as a deer, but the imprinting is not as complete and takes much longer to establish.

Birds are efficient learners, and one might think that this allows us to place them in the hierarchy of evolution. But learning is not a key that can be used for such a purpose. When one looks at the kind of learning to which each species is adapted one can find rapid, efficient learning at all levels of development. For example, A .P. Baerends has demonstrated complex one-trial learning in the solitary digger wasp (Tinbergen, 1951). The wasp digs a hole in the ground, stings a caterpillar and drags it into the nest and lays an egg on it. The egg hatches and the larva eats the caterpillar. The wasp inspects the nest each morning to see how much more caterpillar is needed. She may thus supervise two or even three nests, all at different stages of development, and the provisioning is guided by learning for the wasp first visits all the nests, then goes hunting. An earthworm can learn a Y-maze (Y-shaped, with a single choice point) in 20 trials, about what the laboratory rat needs for the same task. On the other hand, the rat can learn a more complex maze about as fast as human subjects (the rats in an alley maze, the blindfold human subjects with a stylus maze of the same pattern).

It should not really be surprising that higher and lower animals learn equally well when each is presented with a task to which it is suited. (The higher animal's superiority is in learning many more simple things, ones that require more complex responses, and ones depending on more complex relations.) Learning ultimately reduces to synaptic modification, and there is no apparent reason why the modification should take place more slowly in a system of few synapses than in one with many. In fact, the noise problem mentioned above suggests that it should be quicker in the simpler nervous system, and it also appears that the only significant difference in rate of simple learning is that it is slower in the higher animal during infancy: theoretically because experience must first act to organize the transmission paths of the infant brain (the cell-assemblies discussed in Chapter 6).

If the rate of learning is not the key to evolutionary level, what about problem-solving? That after all is directly related to intelligence, and intelligence is what we are concerned with. But there are difficulties here too. The different species differ in sensory and motor equipment as well as in brain capacity. If a dog is better than a rat in a maze-like situation and solves the problem immediately, it may be because of his better vision. The tests that Wolfgang Köhler used to demonstrate insight in the chimpanzee are not suitable for dogs or cats, because they require the primate hand. There is some reason to suspect that the big-brained porpoise, *Tursiops truncatus,* is more highly developed intellectually than the chimpanzee, but there is no possible way of making such a comparison with the two animals in captivity (and the porpoise at least is not likely to be systematically followed and observed in his native habitat, the sea).

Rough comparisons of course are possible, and I do not doubt that the dog is smarter than the rat, or the ape smarter than the dog. Köhler for example showed in *The Mentality of Apes* that the chimpanzee readily sees the possibility of using a box or other object as a stepping-stone to reach a banana hung from the ceiling, but no such behavior has ever been reported for the dog. Though a dog lacks hands to pick up a chair he could push it with a shoulder or drag it with his teeth to where it would allow him to get food otherwise out of reach. This might be awkward, but my point is that the dog does not even see a possibility that is obvious to the chimpanzee. It is a perceptual lack, not motor, and from this point of view it is relevant here to observe that there is a little evidence concerning the development of perceptual capacity in evolution. The laboratory rat, trained to seek food behind a triangle (and not behind a square), does not recognize and respond to the triangle when the figures are rotated from the training position, nor when the figures are black on white instead of white on black as in training. The cat recognizes a rotated triangle, but not one with the color reversal. The chimpanzee recognizes the triangle despite either change—but not when it is made up of six small circles, though a two-year-old human child recognizes this one too.

This and other evidence can be cited if it should be necessary to show that rat, cat, ape and man form an ascending series intellectually, but this is possible only because they are well spaced, separated by long steps. We have no basis for comparing animals closer together in ability, such as cat and dog; such evidence as could be cited would involve learning, which as we have seen has serious limitations—in this case, for example, because dogs have been bred for thousands of years for their readiness to learn. Perhaps dogs are smarter than cats, but it has not been shown to be so. We have no test methods ready by which to appraise the comparative intelligence of the horse for example if that question should be raised, and no basis at all for comparing intelligence in ape and elephant. Neither of these two is at his best in confinement: The Hayes's report of the behavior of their home-reared chimpanzee, Vicki, is enough to show that the cage-reared adults of the Yerkes colony (from which Vicki came) were grossly impaired by being so reared,[8] and reports of the elephant's intelligence, for example in the handling of timber in the Burmese forest under the general direction of his mahout, describe a kind of behavior that could not be studied in a zoo or even in the circus.

The classical test of a capacity for thought in animals is the delayed-response test used by Hunter (1913); as we will see shortly, it does clearly show the presence of representative processes in some animals, but it too is unsatisfactory as a basis of phylogenetic ranking. The length of the delay period, which might have been an index of evolutionary level, does not correlate well with other evidence of ability, small variations of procedure make large differences in the results, and it is not clear how some of these differences are to be interpreted.

The delayed-response procedure however has a fundamental importance. Historically, it was a direct result of behaviorism and Watson's denial of the existence of ideas and imagery. Carr and Hunter appear to have asked themselves what these things mean in terms of behavior. The answer was, acting as if an absent object is still present. When one looks at an object something happens in the brain; if that *something* happens when one is not looking at the object, it is an idea. Thus, Hunter devised a procedure in which the experimental subject was given a sign (a light) to show where food was; the sign was removed (the light was turned off) and after a longer or shorter delay the subject was allowed to go to the food. If he went to the right place the animal was acting as if the light were still shining. Thus he had an idea. Hunter later simplified and improved the procedure by just letting the animal see the food put in one of two containers, then lowering a screen for the delay period to prevent the animal from simply keeping his eyes fixed on the goal. This is the procedure that has been used since that time (about 1917).

The best performances on Hunter's test, by an animal subject, have been obtained from monkeys and apes. In one experiment particularly the evidence of ideation—of the visualization of an object seen earlier but now removed from sight—was obtained in an experiment in Tolman's laboratory by Tinklepaugh (1928). The food his monkeys worked for was sometimes lettuce, which they liked, and sometimes banana, which they liked better. When a monkey saw lettuce being put in one of the food cups and later, when he lifted the lid, found the lettuce, he took it and ate it. But when he saw banana being put in the cup and then found lettuce—Tinklepaugh having made a slight change while the screen was lowered—the monkey's behavior

---

[8]Hayes (1951) and Hayes and Hayes (1952) report behavior by Viki that is so far beyond anything I could elicit from the adults of the Yerkes colony in an attempt I once made to develop an intelligence test for chimpanzees that I can only conclude that the adults were stir-crazy, intellectually impaired not only by rearing in relative restriction but also by the unending monotony of cage life.

was disturbed. He might leave the lettuce and search around and under the cup looking for the missing piece of banana (no other interpretation makes sense). On occasion he had a temper tantrum. This is unambiguous evidence of a representative process, the search and the tantrum resulting from a conflict between expectancy and perception.

There is other evidence of thought in the infrahuman animal. The classical studies of insight by Köhler during the first World War when he was interned on the island of Tenerife are well known and I will not describe them here. Some of his most interesting observations were incidental to his experiments, and the clearest evidence that I know of, of thought and planning by adult chimpanzees, was also provided informally by certain members of the Yerkes colony who liked to spit water on visitors. (The caretaking staff were immune, for water hoses were at hand with which to drench the offender in return.) Even though a visitor was warned to stay at a distance, the chimpanzees looked so innocent and friendly that he would drift insensibly closer as he went from cage to cage, and sooner or later would come within the six-foot range. Now if one was stationed where the chimpanzees could be watched when company was coming one would see a very interesting course of events. An animal who detected the approach of visitors would slip over to the water supply at the back of the cage, fill his mouth, and return to the front of the cage and—when the visitors came near—press himself close to the cage-wire as if inviting contact. There is no doubt of the purposiveness of this behavior, nor or the chimpanzee's enjoyment at the upset behavior of the visitor on being soaked. In other situations the chimpanzee shows capacity for deceit, acting in a way that is normally an invitation to friendly contact until the caretaker or visitor is within reach, then attacking viciously. This is two-stage planning: invitation followed by attack. The water-squirting has *three* stages, getting loaded, attracting the visitor, and soaking him. In the demonstrated abilty to think of doing one thing while actually doing another, or to simulate one attitude while actually having an opposite one, the chimpanzee gives his most convincing evidence of approach to man in mental level.

Let me observe that all this comparative evidence also illuminates the behavior of human beings, quite apart from trying to trace an evolutionary history. From the human data alone one could not guess what an intellectual feat it is to recognize a triangle as such, to see the possibility of using a box as a stepping stone, or still more to think of piling one box on top of another. By human standards the chimpanzee's mechanical achievements are primitive indeed—in piling boxes for example the chimp has no idea of having to center the upper box over the lower, but places it anyhow and may actually climb a structure that he has to hold together as he climbs, his weight on top of the second box being enough to hold it in place—but in comparison with the dog, whose behavior really is at a high level in complexity of function, the chimpanzee takes on a new stature: and man a still higher one, by comparison with the chimpanzee. The comparative perspective gives one respect for the intellectual capacity of the most ordinary of human beings.

EMOTIONS AND MOTIVATIONS

The intellectual gap between man and any other now-existing species is enormous, so much so that if it were not for the anatomical evidence, and the behavioral evidence we will now consider, one would have to be very skeptical indeed about the idea that man and ape or man and elephant share a common ancestor—no matter how far back. The evidence to be considered concerns emotion and motivation and shows a far closer relation between man and ape for example and appears to be so directly connected with an individual animal's intellectual level that we might almost use it as a measure of intelligence.

For this purpose we can again assume that rat, cat or dog, monkey, ape, and man form an ascending series in ability. First, consider anger. In the rat, there is nothing that justifies being classified in this way, as a special form of aggression. The rat will bite if attacked or frightened, and in the case of the female to protect her pups, but there is no sign of the transient attitude of aggression toward another member of the same group that, in higher species, may follow even a minor injury or no injury (think of the tantrum of Tinklepaugh's monkey on finding lettuce when he expected banana), and no sign of jealousy or the peculiar behavior called sulking (whose peculiarity consists in refusing to accept a desired object that had been refused). With the pet dog, *anger* is at times a meaningful term; he is capable of snapping at (not necessarily biting) the child that teases too long, with whom at other times he is on a friendly footing, and he occasionally shows signs of jealousy and even of sulking. When we come to the ape however the term takes on its full meaning. The anger is almost indistinguishable from man's in the variety of causes, in the different ways in which it can be shown, and in its apparent intensity. In addition to the characteristically sudden violent aggression even in response to apparently trivial provocation, the chimpanzee shows jealousy, sulking, and that most interesting phenomenon, the infant temper tantrum—instinctive if there is anything instinctive at this phylogenetic level, since it appears in characteristic form without prior practice and certainly without guidance.

In the Yerkes colony, Kambi always sought attention from any staff member, but would spit at him if he was unwise enough to pay attention to a second animal nearby. Fifi was refused milk (when offered it she had been in the habit of taking a first mouthful and, like a winetaster, rolling it over her tongue and spitting it out before drinking, and the feeder tried to cure her of the wasteful practice), had a tantrum, and then refused for three weeks to take any milk from the one who had refused her, though she would accept it from others after a day or two. A pure fit of the sulks: even a human being could hardly improve on such a specimen. The infant temper tantrum may be recognized at once by any human mother, the baby chimp banging his head on the floor, attempting to pluck handfuls of hair from his body, and apparently choking to death—all the while keeping an eye on mother to see if this is having the desired effect. In the adult animal, rage can be provoked by any of a long list of things that might cause anger in man: persistent noisiness, being startled or teased, importunate begging, a perceived attempt on the part of another to annoy (e. g., Bokar was enraged when Dick, from the next cage, spat water at him even when it did not hit him). Another male had a tantrum repeatedly when a sexually receptive female in a separate cage would not sit where he could gaze on her, the lovely creature; still another had a tantrum at seeing a member of staff take a vaginal smear from a female in heat, though in fact he had often seen the procedure, a routine in a continuing study of the chimpanzee's menstrual cycle. Finally, Bimba liked human beings and was liked by them, but she was also short-tempered and had a way of suspecting that she was being teased if there was any delay in handing over the food at lunch-time and when the feeder's hand came within reach would attack instead of accepting the food. In these causes of anger and in the variety of manifestation there is no apparent evolutionary discontinuity between ape and man.

Nor is there any such discontinuity in the causes of fear, when allowance is made—as we must of course with anger also—for the ape's intellectual level and his lack of language; in man a potent precipitant of both fear and anger. Irrational fears and abhorrences are common in both man and chimpanzee, and remarkably similar in the two species. Man, especially "civilized" man, consistently arranges his affairs so as to limit exposure not only to the possibility of real injury but also to situations that encourage imaginative fears as well as ones that are horrifying or simply nasty. It is extraordinary how readily we forget that fact and how persistently it is left out of account in the discussion of human nature and human society. The chimpanzee we regard as a wild animal, man as in a sense domesticated, tame, unemotional; but this is ethnocentric blindness. The chimpanzee on his own ground is not perceptually excited, as Jane Goodall's work shows; and his "wildness" in captivity amounts to objecting to physical restraint, as well as readiness to use force if opportunity offers when he wants his own way. None of this makes him different from man, and in certain respects we may—almost—use him as a mirror in which to see certain characteristics of our own species.

Adult chimpanzees fear snakes when they have had no injury from them, not even physical contact, and of course they have not been told that snakes are dangerous. The infant fears strangers (this "shyness" begins at about four months, about six months in the human baby) and if he is brought up in the nursery and is used to three or four persons only, the disturbance may be great. The adult avoids small animals or, if escape is not possible, attacks viciously. An adult female was greatly disturbed at finding a worm in the biscuit she was eating. These various susceptibilities clearly show a kinship with man. Now we come to one in which the relation may not be evident at once—but only because we keep on forgetting the existence of certain human characteristics.

In an accidental observation I found that the adults of the Yerkes colony were panic-stricken at the sight of a model of a chimpanzee head. The model was in clay, about half life-size, made only to discover whether the chimpanzees would be more interested in a three-dimensional representation of a familar object than in a two-dimensional one. I was astonished at what I saw when this innocent object was presented to their view. Some of them screamed, defecated, fled from their outer cages to the inner rooms where they were not within sight of the clay model; those that remained in sight stood at the back of the cage, their gaze fixed on the model held in my hand. None would approach. Subsequent tests showed that this was a generalized response to any object recognizably representing a part of the chimpanzee or the human body, including an actual chimpanzee head that had been preserved in formalin; a model human head, very lifelike, from a display dummy and a human hand taken from the same source; and a plaster cast from a death-mask of another chimpanzee that died about this time. With repeated testing the strength of the response decreased, but none of the animals ever approached and touched one of these objects, and a doll—a representation of a naked human baby—was put in the same cage with some of the adults and, despite the well-known tendency of the chimpanzee to investigate destructible objects by taking them to pieces, the doll remained untouched.

A further point, also of great interest. The emotionality is a function of age. One and two-year-old animals paid no attention to the model head. They simply begged to be picked up when a familiar attendant approached with it in his hand. Five and six-year-olds however were fascinated by it—but unlike their elders, wanted to get a close as possible and would undoubtedly have taken it to pieces if they had got a chance.

As I have said, the emotional response of the adult chimpanzee seems at first sight to be mysterious, unlike anything we have known about, but if one considers the intellectual level of the chimpanzee and still more what the exciting objects represented—namely, parts of the body—there is a parallel to be found. This is in the attitude of human beings brought up in a sheltered environment (as the chimpanzees in question also were) to the sight of surgical operations and dismembered bodies. Watching even a color film of an open-heart operation causes fainting. The dead body has some of the same emotion-provoking properties; no one in this society is likely to admit being afraid of the dead, but actual fear is evident in the elaborate ritual that in many societies is or used to be necessary to propitiate the spirits of the dead, and if that fear does not exist in our own society we still take remarkable care to limit exposure to the dead body and to ritualize the procedures for dealing with it. The parallel between chimpanzee and man is more marked when it is recalled also that the human young, like the young chimpanzees, tend not to be disturbed by the sight of flowing blood, talk about broken bodies in air crashes, and gruesome tales of witches who eat little children and wolves swallowing grandma. As adults we read these "children's stories" to five-year-olds without a qualm, but, it seems, only because we ourselves became familiar with them at a less sensitive if not more bloodthirsty age. It also reminds us that the usual adult sensitivity does not appear when the child has grown up exposed to bloodshed, just as the child who plays with snakes and continues to do so during later childhood is likely to be immune to the otherwise universal horror of harmless as well as poisonous snakes. The chimpanzee data clearly show that the fear need not be learned; on the contrary, it is *not* fearing snakes that must be learned.

In all this, it is evident that there is a close relation between intellectual level and the emotional susceptibility that we have been considering. It is the higher animal that is more disturbed and vulnerable to the wider range of provocations; and, in a given species, the older rather than the younger. This runs counter to common sense, which sees the human five-year-old as the excitable one, not his father or mother. But there is an answer to such objections. The child's emotionality appears mostly when he is being made to conform to adult requirements: the adult's lack of emotionality is mostly dependent on living in an environment that is particularly suited to adult sensitivities, and the adult has also had long practice in not giving free rein to the emotions that do occur even in that sheltered environment.

How is a relation between intellectual level and susceptibility to emotional disturbance to be understood? Obviously a contributing factor is the greater ability of the higher animal compared to the lower, or of the adult compared to the child, to detect danger, to perceive another's malice or intent to obstruct, or to realize that one has made oneself ridiculous. A closely related factor is the greater capacity for imagining danger or malice or ridicule where it does not exist. Thus shame is not something known to the two-year-old, for example, and fear of the dark tends not to appear till the age of three and is stronger at four and five when the child is more capable of imagining monsters in the bedroom shadows. But this is still not the whole story.

In a simple analogy, we might think of emotional disturbance as a momentary breakdown of the orderly normal functioning of the brain (often followed, it is true, by well-organized flight or attack, but momentarily disruptive nonetheless). The more complex a piece of equipment the more ways its smooth functioning can be impaired, and so with the more elaborate thought process of the adult higher animal. This is analogy only, but there is a fundamentally noncognitive, unreasoning element in some of these emotions. A good example is the powerful fear or horror aroused by snakes. An adult can be convinced that a nonpoisonous snake is harmless and still find it so abhorrent that he cannot bring himself to touch it, let alone pick it up.[9] There is no rational basis for that avoidance. In some way the limbless writhing, the lack of hair or feathers, and the mysterious movement over the ground without benefit of legs—between them, it seems that these set up an intrinsically *perceptual* conflict, or conflict of percept with preexistent concepts of animals and animal movement. Similarly, the emotional upset at the sight of a surgical operation has nothing cognitive as its cause. One might argue that the equally strong upset at the sight of an autopsy or the dissection of a cadaver is the result of knowing that we all must die—that it is in other words a fear of dying, somewhat displaced. But this cannot account for the reaction to the surgical operation, whose function is to maintain life, and it certainly cannot account for fainting on seeing a badly lacerated hand being sewn up or for the frequently emotional reaction to the sight of a badly disfigured face—or even the stump of an amputated arm or leg.

A physiological clue to this surprising relation between intellect and emotionality comes from the discovery about 1950 of the role of the ascending reticular activating system (ARAS), or arousal system, low in the brain stem, in the maintenance of thought and consciousness. This also has the value of relating the negative or disruptive emotions that I have talked about so far to the positive and integrative emotions such as joy and love. My emphasis on anger and fear, in the preceding, is not because they are more important but because they provide most of our evidence. They are easier to observe and record because they often appear as a sharp break in the ongoing flow of behavior. (Harlow's 1971 fundamentally important study of love provides formal experimental evidence concerning one of the positive emotions, but it does not make species comparisons, which is our present concern.) I have no doubt that friendship, regarded as a nonsexual, nonparental attachment to another member of the species, is a mark of the higher animal and of the older rather than the younger animal, but there is little evidence to cite in support, apart from the fact that it is prominent in human behavior and the fact that strongly established friendships have been observed in chimpanzees and porpoises (McBride & Hebb, 1948).

---

[9]Jones and Jones (1928) reported the behavior of younger and older human subjects exposed to a harmless and torpid snake. All were city-dwellers and had had no contact with snakes. They were also shown that the snake was in fact harmless. Avoidance increased with age from about 6 to 16, and the older teen-aged subjects were unwilling to make any contact with it.

The arousal system, deep in the brain stem, is relevant because as Lindsley (1951) has pointed out it is essentially involved in emotional behavior. There are cognitive elements in emotion also, and the limbic system is involved as well as the arousal system, but it is the arousal system that puts the energy into an emotional response. Its activity is necessary if the cortex is to function at all, and it is not unreasonable to suppose that its role increases in importance as the cortex becomes bigger and its operations become more complex. On this basis we can understand a close relation between intelligence and emotionality.

A relation between positive and negative emotions also appears. It seems that there is an optimal level of arousal; below this level, the subject tends to act so as to raise it, above it he tends to act so as to reduce it. The positive emotions are found in the lower and middle parts of the range, the negative emotions in the upper part. The positive emotions are states in which the subject tries to maintain contact with the stimulating object or situation, to achieve closer contact, or to make repeated contact. The stimulation, in short, is desirable. The negative emotions are reactions to undesirable stimulation. They are states in which the subject tries to change the stimulating conditions (by attack, in rage, or by avoidance), or ones like grief in which the subject has no control over the stimulating conditions (absence due to death, e.g.). Oversimplifying somewhat, a low level of arousal is boredom and the subject seeks excitement; a moderate level is the norm in waking behavior and tends to maintain itself and the concurrent behavior; and a high level tends to take a form of rage or fear and interrupt (at least momentarily) the behavior leading up to it. A qualification is that different kinds of behavior may tolerate, so to speak, different levels of arousal: a 100-yard dash, for example, is itself a form of violence, not requiring any subtlety of cortical function, and so arousal may be high without doing anything but support the behavior. It also seems clear that there are different forms of arousal to be taken account of. Another qualification is that very high levels of arousal may result in a prolonged impairment of thought (i.e., more than seconds in duration) and even the motor impairment of the so-called paralysis of terror.

How the arousal system has its psychological effects is still conjecture. We know that its activity is necessary for transmission of sensory messages through the cortex, and for the interaction of cortical systems. We may suppose then that in an unexciting situation any stimulation that raises the level of arousal will be responded to selectively, maintaining the arousal; also, the cortex can excite the arousal system, as well as vice versa, so an exciting thought can take control of behavior and result in a seeking out of excitation. However, when arousal is still higher, cortical transmission and excitability may be too much increased. Cortical processes that interfere with or inhibit one another may occur simultaneously and disrupt the behavior that led up to that situation. As for "paralysis," this is something that is sometimes observed in persons who suddenly and unexpectedly find themselves in a dangerous situation calling for immediate action. It may take the form of an actual inability to move, or an equally fatal inability to think clearly or to decide on a course of action (Tyhurst, 1951).

Different forms of arousal are seen, for example, in anger and in laughter, and it appears that these result from different patterns of firing in the arousal system. In fear and anger the sympathetic nervous system is excited, and the aftereffects of the arousal last for some time. In laughter the momentary effect may be just as strong ("helpless with laughter") but there is little of the autonomic aftereffect. The arousal system consists of some 28 separate pairs of nuclei, which makes possible different patterns of activity, all with the same function of activating the cortex but with different properties otherwise.

ALTRUISM

Finally, let us consider altruism as another mark of the higher animal and a product of evolution. It is a distinguishing mark of the human species. As we will see, it is not unique to man, but it is common in all human societies, ranging from the very frequent acts of small assistance to occasional risk and even loss of life. A widely held view is that human generosity is really selfishness (due to fear of social censure, or the reward of social approval), or possibly a closely related form of stupidity (having been punished as a child for greed, the adult does not fully realize that he is now free from such control). Another basis for asserting that generosity or kindness is really selfish is to argue that the giver gets pleasure from giving, the rescuer from rescuing, and so on. This is nothing but a play on words. It leaves unaffected the real distinction between helping and not helping, between those who can get their kicks in this way and those who cannot. For our present purposes, it means only that we redefine altruism as a tendency to help others without *external* reward (and of course not because of fear of being punished if one does not help). It is most easily understood as a product of empathy, the partial identification with another that has already been discussed (p. 24).

There is unambiguous evidence of a disinterested (but not *un*interested) concern for others in the porpoise and the chimpanzee, though the evidence is more complete for the chimpanzee reared in captivity since his history can be known from birth.

The story of the porpoise's contacts with man is fascinating and depressing: fascinating in itself and because what had been thought to be ancient myth, uncritically recorded by Aristotle, Pliny and others of the classical era, has suddenly been made factual; depressing because human promoters have found out how to cash in on the fascination by imprisoning this intelligent, friendly and sensitive animal in small pools all over the country, for human entertainment and promoter's profit.

The story is recorded by Kellogg (1961), together with a report of the extraordinary ability of the porpoise, like that of the bat, to perceive and identify objects by hearing or "echolocation"; and by Alpers (1961), who records in detail the story of Opo, the young female porpoise that came into the shallow waters of the beach at Opononi, New Zealand, in 1955, to make friends with a young lady named Jill Baker and to play with her and the other bathers: full confirmation of Pliny's tale of similar friendships in the Mediterranean in classical times.

The evidence of concern for others includes help given by porpoises to other porpoises, which is not disputed, but also help given to human swimmers in trouble, whose meaning at least *is* disputed. First, the help to other porpoises: A female giving birth in the pool of Marine Studios in Florida was surrounded by other females in a clearly protective way (McBride & Hebb, 1948). They warded off an aggressive male and a shark attracted by the blood in the water. When the newborn infant began a first slow gradual ascent to the surface to breathe, a second female accompanied the mother in swimming just below the infant in a position to give support if it had failed to reach the surface. There is no doubt that the porpoise understands the need of other porpoises to reach the air (the animal's own rising to the surface is not merely reflexive and noncognitive). If an infant is sick or does not swim, the mother will support it at the surface, continuing to do so for some time, and it is known that adults will give similar support to other adults. Siebenaler and Caldwell (1956) have recorded two examples. In one a porpoise in a school was stunned by the explosion of a stick of dynamite nearby; in the other a captured porpoise was accidentally struck on the head as he was being lowered into a holding tank. Both times two other animals came immediately to the stunned animal's assistance, one on each side under a pectoral fin (Figure 8) to hold him up till he could swim again. It is of interest to note that such aid from a single animal would have been no good, since it would simply tilt the unconscious animal over so that the blow-hole would be submerged; the dual effort constitutes a higher level of intelligent cooperation than anything recorded for that animal genius, the chimpanzee.

This evidence of help spontaneously and promptly given to others in trouble, with its evidence of an understanding of the need of air by other porpoises at least, should be kept in mind when we consider the reports of aid given to human beings in trouble in the water. The classical tales of rescue in the Mediterranean may have originated with real events (in view of the two modern incidents reported in the following) but they show signs of fanciful elaboration due to word-of-mouth transmission. They have become folklore (unlike Pliny's circumstantial accounts of boy-porpoise friendship), but the fact that they exist at all and were widely believed by those who knew the

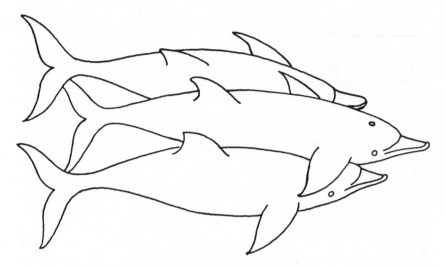

FIG. 8.   Sketch of two porpoises supporting another, one on each side. From Siebenaler and Caldwell (1956).

animals may carry some weight. However, Kellogg (1961) provides two modern instances of help by porpoises to human swimmers. A woman bather was caught in an undertow and was swept under water, could not regain control, and was losing consciousness when she was bumped violently and found herself in shallower water where she could stand up. A man who had seen this told her that when he arrived she looked like a dead body in the water and that she was shoved ashore by a porpoise (which was still present, near the beach). Another woman fell overboard at night and was twice nudged away from adverse currents by a porpoise that stayed close till the swimmer could stand up "and then took off like a streak on down the channel."

An undue fear of anthropomorphizing—reading human attitudes and purposes into animal behavior without justification—can easily lead to the opposite error, of refusing to recognize the plain meaning of infrahuman behavior that happens to go beyond the observer's narrow view of what an animal is capable of. The difficulty, in the two cases above, may be either a low estimate of porpoise intelligence or a disbelief in the possibility of altruism toward members of another species, that is, human beings. In view of the whole record of porpoise behavior, neither is a good basis of skepticism.

For the chimpanzee, the evidence of altruistic behavior is clear. I do not of course suggest that altruism is necessarily more frequent than selfishness, whether in man, porpoise, or chimp, but argue only that it does occur. In the Yerkes colony it had been observed that an animal possessing food might give some of it to a hungry neighbor, and Nissen and Crawford (1936) put this tendency to experimental test. They found that when two chimpanzees were friends, the one with food would share freely; when they were not friends the "rich" animal might still find the other's begging irresistible, and so give less— but still give.

A more dramatic evidence of concern for another's welfare appeared in an experimental study of the chimpanzee's attitude toward human beings, and the effect of a visitor's boldness or timidity (Hebb & Thompson, 1968). The experimenter when disguised as the Bold Man, wearing heavy gloves and safely outside the cage wire, simply acted as one with no fear of chimpanzees. If the chimp was friendly, so was he, but he took no nonsense from others. In one cage were two close friends, Lia and Mimi. Lia was wary of the Bold Man but Mimi attacked (i.e., tried to scratch or bite). The Bold Man replied in kind, catching one of Mimi's fingers through the wire mesh and bending it back slightly, enough to hurt. Mimi screamed with rage, beat on the cage wire, and tried again to catch a finger of the Bold Man. Lia was also angry when Mimi was hurt and joined in the attack, but was frightened off by the apparent vigor of the Bold Man's responses. Having retreated to the back of the cage, evidently afraid, she nevertheless returned—not to re-enter the fight but to try to pull the reckless Mimi away and prevent her from attacking the Bold Man. When the test was repeated in later weeks Lia showed less emotional excitement but continued to work at getting Mimi out of trouble. Observers thoroughly familiar with the animals of the colony were left with no doubt: Lia was afraid, but also feared for Mimi and was willing to run some risk to get her out of the danger zone.

It is extraordinary how strong the tradition is that selfishness is the only credible motivation—extraordinary, that is, in view of all the human experience to the contrary. The attitude long antedates Darwin, but it was reinforced when evolution came to be regarded as a process of "survival of the fittest" (and by implication, survival of the most selfish). Sharing food in times of famine, or trying to rescue a drowning swimmer, can only make one's own survival less likely. Such behavior occurs, however, and is not really the exception in such situations.

With the development of genetics in this century the problem becomes more specific. One may say that it is not the individual that is the significant variable in evolution, but the family or tribe or species, and the gene pool; a gene pool that throws up some proportion of individuals prone to help others may survive better than one that does not, which is obviously true where parental behavior is concerned. Without that instinctive pattern of behavior no bird or mammal would now exist. The question is, however, what evolutionary mechanism can it be that produces such a situation in the first place? Apart from parental behavior, one might see how with learning cooperative tendencies might be maintained once established, but how would that state of affairs originate?

For part of the problem a relatively direct mechanism is available from genetic theory. This deals with parental behavior and supportive behavior between siblings. Relatives have genes in common, so the support given to one's kin, though it does not favor one's own survival does mean that those genes of one's own that produce such behavior will survive, transmitted by kin—so the behavior reappears in the next generation. But this does not apply to supporting behavior given to ones outside the family. Here there is another variable for the geneticist to take account of.

Wilson (1975) in *Sociobiology* as well as others have confused the issue by failing to consider the differences of behavioral control in the worker ant and in the higher mammals. The "altruism" of the ant is reflexive, noncognitive, genetically programmed given a normal environment. The altruism of chimpanzee and man is cognitive, conscious, and idea-controlled, and it is with respect to this behavior in the higher animal that the problem of true altruism arises. A directly genetic explanation of the behavior of the sterile ant's supportive behavior can be accepted (and also presumably for the strongly instinctive and more or less compulsive maternal behavior of bird and mammal) but we can look elsewhere for explanation of the evolution of true altruism. The idea in short is that this is a by-product, not something with direct evolutionary value but a consequence of something else that does have such value—namely, a high intelligence and the capacity for thought.

We have seen in Chapter 2 that there is strong behavioral evidence for the existence of empathy, the identification of self with other, in chimpanzee as well as in man. It was also seen that there is a theoretical rationale for such a state of affairs, to be found in the fact that the infant must first develop an idea of a person from the perception of others and develop an idea of self only on that basis. Thus the idea of the self and the other have a common core. In favorable circumstances, then, learning that is based on self-interest may with suitable modification transfer to support for another. This is of course not inevitable, just as altruism is not a universal feature of human behavior; the necessary "suitable modification," the fact that the actual response is not the same in helping another as in helping oneself, may account for the fact that the response is often not made. But the fact also is at the cognitive level that "sympathy," and the *idea* of help, is very common indeed. That it is often compelling is evident in human society; and the same thing can be true of the chimpanzee, when an animal with food is subjected to continued begging by another and finally gives in—by throwing the food violently at the beggar, apparently unable to resist.

One still encounters that assertion that true altruism in human beings is not possible, whatever may hold for the ant and the bee. It is implied that generosity is a kind of artificial addition made in childhood; and by the time maturity is reached the human being has done some complex learning, making it practically impossible to show that this is not really so. When one is faced with the flat assertion that altruism is not possible however, the animal data are there to rebut the assertion. In the case of the chimpanzee at least the evidence is clear, that altruism can appear spontaneously, and we need no longer shut our eyes to the fact of kindness—sporadic kindness at least—as an outstanding characteristic of the human species. Meanness and cruelty are species characteristics also, it is true, but they are not the whole story.

5

Heredity, the IQ, and Attendant Confusions

In this modern and enlightened day a chapter on the heredity-environment question may look like flogging a dead horse. Unfortunately, the horse is not dead. I hope with luck to make this chapter short but, long or short, it is still needed.

There are vital social and educational as well as theoretical issues that are widely misunderstood, not because they are so complex in principle but because of the persistence of old habits of thought. An unfortunate result is that well-meaning people, concerned to support the deprived, white as well as black, sometimes take positions that tend to injure istead of support. In this biological-psychological problem area even the biological scientist may become confused in dealing with behavior, clear as he is about morphology. As for the social scientist, his simple preference seems to be to abrogate all the laws of genetics as they apply to differences between human beings.

William James once referred to a certain misconception about self-knowledge as "the psychologist's fallacy." The psychologist's fallacy today is to suppose that all behavioral problems are problems of learning, and to forget—or deny—the significance of heredity and constitution. There are social scientists, including many psychologists, who believe and are prepared to state publicly that, barring birth injury, all members of the human race are born not merely equal but identical, apart from such trivia as muscular strength and agility, sex organs, skin color, and the like; the differences of ability and of propensity or motivation that are so marked at maturity are all products of experience during growth. Even more, it has become fashionable to deplore research in this area, clearly with the problem of race relations in mind and the entirely false notion that the research has been injurious to the

American black. As we will see, the truth is exactly opposite, certain current aberrations to the contrary notwithstanding.

The idea that all is learning and that human differences are all a question of an acquired personality—the motivations and self-image that originate in the experiences of childhood—that idea is to be found in the discussion of matters as widely separate as obesity and Women's Liberation. There is research that blames obesity on a love of food—that is, on greed—with no apparent recognition of a continuing need produced by the underlying physiological disorder; in general, being overweight is regarded as the result of eating too much and exercising too little—with no recognition of the genetic variable that makes it impossible for some of us to gain weight and makes it inevitable for others. Likewise, alcoholism is really regarded as self-indulgence, despite lip service to the idea that it is an illness. There is a constitutional variable here too. In effect some people are no more capable of becoming alcoholics than a skinny woman is of getting a little fatter, much as she might like to; for others the addiction can be established only too readily. The difference presumably appears in the immediacy and degree of pleasure that is derived from alcohol, and the beginner who finds great enjoyment in a drinking party might do well to regard that fact as a warning. He is not likely to do so however if he takes for granted that all men are born equal (constitutionally, with respect to alcohol) and, seeing others drink freely without becoming drunks, takes for granted that he can too.

From this same egalitarian point of view, *mental illness* is a misnomer, and there are psychologists, many of them, who are indignant at any suggestion that neurosis or psychosis is a medical problem, to be treated in the first place by one with medical training—that is, by a psychiatrist. The idea instead is that such disorders arise from experience and constitute only a problem of re-education. Now if there is one thing in this field that has been established in the past 30 years or so it is that there are genetic factors in the common psychoses, which must have a biochemical basis, and that both neurosis and psychosis are better treated with chemotherapy (tranquillizers, anti-depressants) than without. But let us not go to extremes. That statement does not deny importance to psychotherapy and behavior-modification methods. Not all disorders have a special biochemical component, and in those that do psychotherapy may still have great value though by itself it does not cure.

The egalitarian tendency in feminism shows up, uncontrolled, in those writers who deny any inborn psychological differences between male and female. The differences between adult men and women are all products of social pressure. The tendency is also evident in those who recognize the existence of a genetic component but are concerned to keep it to a minimum and put the burden of proof on the hereditarian. No great weight is given to biological evidence from other species, even when it favors the female: leadership by the female contrasted with dominance among males, in deer, for example, or the apparently greater social intelligence and courage of the female chimpanzee (Hebb & Thompson, 1968).

THE BIOLOGIST'S FALLACY

The biologist has a fallacy too, though I hasten to say that just as the psychologist's fallacy is shared with sociologists and other social scientists, so the biologist is far from being in sole possession of his. The biologist's fallacy is to ask whether a given character is inherited or acquired. In that form today it is rare except when dealing with behavior and even then is more likely to take the form of asking *how much* some aspect of behavior depends on heredity and how much on environment, or *how important* heredity or environment is for the behavior. But either question is bad; the only answer is that any behavior depends fully on both variables, that both are of hundred-percent importance. The relation between them is not additive, so that as one becomes more important the other becomes less; instead, one depends fully on the other. In an analogy used elsewhere, heredity and environment are related to behavior as length and breadth of a field are related to its area. To say that human intelligence is 80% heredity, 20% environment—or that it depends more on heredity than on environment—is to make the biologist's fallacy. It is like saying that the area of the field depends more on its length than on its width. Heredity by itself, or the fertilized ovum at the moment of conception, can produce no intellligence whatsoever. Its potential can be realized only with the conjoined environmental action of the uterus until birth and a supporting postnatal environment for some time after that. And *vice versa*: The environment can do nothing without a fertilized ovum to work on.

There is also a tendency to forget how varied the different modes of environmental action are and even, when dealing with intelligence, to reduce the all effects of environment to learning—and at that, a kind of learning that is known only in the half-grown or adult organism. As we will see, the infant's first learning is of a different kind and needs to be taken account of separately.

The accompanying table is a means of keeping things clear. It is a mnemonic rather than a logically tight analysis (e.g., the genetic factor in behavior is the DNA carried by the ovum, not the ovum as a whole) but precise enough to serve its purpose. Factor I then is (roughly) heredity. Factors II and III are the normally supportive physical environment, distinguished because Factor II, prenatal, is sometimes forgotten but should not be: Malnutrition in the mother for example can have serious effects, and so can her use of drugs. Factors IV and V are both experiential, but here again a distinction is important. Factor IV, exposure to the normal sensory environment of the young of the species, has very often been forgotten, and

TABLE 1.
CLASSES OF FACTORS IN BEHAVIORAL DEVELOPMENT[a]

No.	Class	Source, Mode of Action, etc.
I	genetic	physiological properties of the fertilized ovum
II	chemical, prenatal	nutritive or toxic influence in the uterine environment
III	chemical, postnatal	nutritive or toxic influence: food, water, oxygen, drugs, etc.
IV	sensory, constant	pre- and postnatal experience normally inevitable for all members of the species
V	sensory, variable	experience that varies from one member of the species to another
VI	traumatic	physical events tending to destroy cells: an "abnormal" class of events to which an animal might conceivably never be exposed. unlike Factors I to V

[a]From Hebb (1972). By permission.

some of the learning it induces is different from, and prerequisite to, the learning that occurs later in development. This is true both theoretically and empirically. *Theoretically,* the first learning is the slow development of cell-assemblies which, once developed, make possible the faster—often one-trial—learning of maturity, as a changed relation between assemblies. *Empirically,* infant learning is slower and completely lacks insight; it must begin in very early infancy and cannot be replaced by later learning, at least not fully; without it, adult personality and intelligence are grossly defective (e.g., when dog or monkey is reared in isolation in the laboratory, or the human baby is reared in what amounts to isolation in certain orphanages).

The codification of these factors in development has the immediate value of making it impossible to think of behavior as determined by any one variable. It also clarifies terms. Thus, reflex behavior is a product of Factors I to III; instinctive behavior, especially in the higher animal, brings in Factor IV as well (instinctive behavior is no longer thought to be wholly unlearned but depends also on the learning that comes from simple exposure to the common environment). Intelligent behavior likewise is a product of Factors I to IV, but whereas instinctive behavior is evoked by features usual in the common environment, intelligent behavior is evoked by the unusual, and so involves the stimulation of Factor V. Factor V is also the source of the learning that differs from one animal or person to another, but it must be emphasized that Factor V alone can do nothing: For all cognitive learning Factor IV is necessary, and Factors I to III are necessary for any learning whatsoever. Here it may be seen also that behavior may be unlearned, in the usual sense of the word, and still be dependent on prior learning. An insightful or an instinctive action is unlearned since it does not result from practice or instruction or observation of another's performance, and yet it requires the Factor-IV learning normal to the species.

THE IQ AND ITS VALUES

The in thing today in the discussion of intelligence is to talk about *the heritability of the IQ,* but not always with comprehension of the limits of the meaning of that statistical conception. Heritability is the proportion of the variance that results from differences of heredity. It is not easily determined for the IQ, so estimates differ. It has been common to arrive at a figure of .80 (80% of the variance), but on the other hand one egalitarian has tried to show that it is about zero—concluding that one's heredity has nothing to do with one's intelligence.

That extreme view, and at the other extreme, the idea that high heritability would mean that environmental modification can have little effect on the IQ—specifically, on the mean IQ of U.S. blacks—is adequately dealt with in the outstanding monograph by Loehlin, Lindzey, and Spuhler (1975). The book is outstanding in its treatment of race and the uncertainties that enter into the interpretation of a figure for the heritability of the IQ, and what heritability means or does not mean in the comparison of black and white.

On one point I believe they should be clearer: in the reference of that term *intelligence,* which in the psychological literature sometimes means, approximately, the goodness of the infant brain (or at an even earlier stage, the quality of the genetic contribution thereto), and sometimes means the level of intellectual function that is achieved at maturity. That is, the term sometimes refers to genotype, sometimes to phenotype. In the past I have distinguished between the two meanings as *intelligence A* and *intelligence B,* and I believe to avoid confusion the distinction is still necessary.

Intelligence in sense *A* cannot be measured; it is an even more inferential entity than other psychological variables, which are also inferred from behavior. Intelligence in sense *B* however is quite measurable, with relatively short steps of inference by tests which in effect sample a cultural product, to determine the extent to which the person being tested has mastered the ideas, modes of thought and of solving problems, ways of perceiving, and the store of information characteristic of the society for which the test is standardized. Thus the idea of a culture-free test is a contradiction, and in fact the test items that predict best are "Binet-type" items: ones so culture-loaded that they offer no difficulty for those who can succeed with them at all. They are not problems because, in effect, they merely ask for solutions that the subject has already worked out, and what he has already learned in the ordinary course of experience. Thus the test does not pose a set of new problems to be solved here and now. Solving new problems might seem more logical for an intelligence test, but in fact it works poorly; what Binet really discovered was that the level or quality of mental function *in the past* is the best predictor for the future. The so-called culture-free tests are neither culture-free nor predict well. The Raven Matrices test for example makes ingenious use of a certain kind of logical operation, nonverbal and independent of any specific past experience, but it is not the test by which to find out how well a child from the slums is prepared for school.

On the other hand, the idea of a culture-*fair* test is simply confused. In what respect can a Stanford-Binet orWechsler test be unfair? Only as an index of intelligence *A* in cases where the environment has been deficient—that is, as an index of native ability. But no test can measure intelligence *A*. The question is simply, How well does the test predict? *The same conditions that impair the IQ also impair clerical and academic aptitude,* so a Wechsler rating would predict about as well for a Stone-Age Indian as for a New Yorker if one wanted to know how well either would do in a business office in the city or at Columbia University. (The only qualification concerns the subject who does not speak English but who grew up in a similar Western-European culture. As he learns English his test score rises, but so does intelligence *B,* his effectiveness in an English-speaking business or academic world, so the short-term prediction at least is valid, if the long-term one is not.)

The IQ is in bad odor today. It is said to be racist and unjust and a means of further oppressing the oppressed, all of which is completely wrong. If the results are abused the abuse should be corrected, but the intelligence test is a tool of the greatest potential importance, for the disadvantaged student particularly. It should be recognized that the IQ is essentially an academic *diagnosis*, an estimate of the child's probable rate of learning the kind of thing that a school wants him to learn. The diagnosis has a known probable error, but the error is least where the diagnosis is most important—that is, with low IQs—and it helps in adjusting the course of study to the needs of the individual. Too often the slower learner who is not obviously destined for a special school for the retarded is simply dropped into the main stream under pressure to keep up with the average, which he cannot do. He becomes frustrated and unhappy and learns to hate everything connected with school. Formerly, he failed examinations annually and repeated grades and quit school as soon as he could manage it; today, examinations (like the IQ) are considered discriminatory, and in the name of egalitarian principles the slower learner is likely to be promoted year after year without examination and so ends up in high school unable to read—when with some adjustment of the curriculum he might have got at least the beginning of an education.

Similarly, the bad name of research on intelligence is undeserved. Those liberal thinkers who would dissuade us from it clearly think it will turn out badly—that is, that it will support the idea that the black citizen is genetically inferior. But there is no reason to expect that result, and the whole force of research has been to the contrary.

Consider the U.S. Army data of 1918. There is little doubt that in the nineteenth century the black was regarded as intrinsically inferior; to be convinced one need only look at some of Abraham Lincoln's talk about how one might deal with the newly freed slaves when the Civil War would be over. The first big dent in that attitude was made by the report of Robert M. Yerkes (1921) and his colleagues on the result of testing American recruits in the first world war. Instead of finding the black scores to be a separate distribution, massed below the white, they found a great overlap, a significant proportion of blacks making better scores than a significant portion of whites. A myth at that point was shown to be nothing but a myth—by psychological research.

The research then went on to make a further contribution by showing how dependent test performance is upon the subject's social background. This seems to have been generally regarded as a defect of the available tests, and it was at that stage that various attempts were made to develop a culture-free intelligence test—not realizing that the environmental effect might go deeper and affect intelligence itself (intelligence B, that is) as well as the IQ. That further realization came with animal studies in which rearing conditions could be completely controlled, using as experimental subjects the laboratory rat (Hymovitch, 1952) and Scottish terriers (Thompson & Heron, 1954). This, and perhaps also the provision of a theoretical rationale—the necessity of experience to develop cell-assemblies that are the basis of intelligence—threw a new light on human data that already existed. Gordon (1928) and Asher (1935) had reported losses of 25 to 30 points of IQ after the age of about 5 years, the former in the canal-boat children of England, the latter in the Kentucky Mountain children: The data imply that the environmental stimulation was adequate for cognitive growth in the first years of life, inadequate thereafter. William Goldfarb's (1943) unique data in particular were decisive. He showed that three years in an orphanage, about the ages of one to three, resulted in a mean IQ of 72 in comparison with a mean of 95 for a matched group placed at the same ages in foster homes, the test being given some years later between the ages of 10 and 12. At this time Beth Wellman (1940) and her colleagues were trying to convince others that improving the environment could raise the IQ of deprived children, and met ridicule. The animal data changed that situation completely.

All this work should have made it clear that the IQ and intelligence B are both vulnerable to the effects of an impoverished environment, and where the blacks are concerned that their lower mean IQ—10 to 15 points lower—may be low for that reason only. But it should also be clear that intelligence A is removed by too many steps of inference from the observed IQ for us ever to be able to compare it in any two socially distinct groups in the country.

WHAT A HIGH HERITABILITY DOES NOT MEAN

It is evident that some psychologists (and it seems some biologists) still think in an unacceptable older way about heritability; if heritability is high, little modification of the phenotype will be made by manipulation of the environment, and the phenotype mirrors the genotype. The falsity of such ideas is emphasized by Loehlin, Lindzey, and Spuhler, and even more vigorously by Feldman and Lewontin(1975). But the inertia of that older way of thinking about heredity and environment is great, and the argument may become more effective if it is translated into concrete terms. Hence the two following thought-experiments.

T-experiment A: Let us suppose that some miraculous new development of genetic engineering makes it possible to provide all infants of the next generation with a first-class, high-quality set of the genes that contribute to the development of intelligent behavior. When this is done, all having the same genetic constitution in that respect, everyone's intellectual endowment will be the same but, since the children must be brought up by their present parents and in very different environments, their behavior will vary considerably. What about the heritability of the IQ once these children have grown up and society consists of them and their children? Heritability is the proportion of the variance that is determined by variations of heredity, but there is no variation of heredity, so the result of a profoundly important hereditary modification is to reduce heritability to zero—but this obviously does not mean that the importance of heredity is reduced.

T-experiment B: Mark Twain once proposed that all boys should be brought up in barrels and fed through the bung-hole till the age of 12. Let us imagine that his advice was taken and has been followed since then. The result today is that there is a big gap between the intelligence of men and women; and the women, who now staff the universities and run the country, ask themselves scientifically what to do about the abysmally low male IQ. In the best academic tradition they determine its heritability first. This turns out to be very high indeed, since the environment during growth is practically identical for all males and cannot contribute to the variance of the male IQ. If the female scientists are among those for whom high heritability means that the environment is not an important cause, they will see no reason not to go on rearing boys in barrels.

Heritability is a descriptive statistic that has limited value as an analytical tool with which to investigate the complex relation of heredity to environment in the mechanisms of behavior. High heritability of the IQ does not lessen the importance of the environment as a determinant of behavior, nor show that the IQ in a segment of the population has not been depressed by adverse conditions during infancy.

On the other hand, it does show that the genetic variable is also a source of variability of the IQ. Put in the crudest terms, it shows that some children inherit better brains than other children, and it is really this crude proposition that is offensive to the egalitarian attitude to which I referred in the early part of this chapter. In the attempt to refute it, some extraordinary illogic has been indulged in by otherwise intelligent people. One pair of critics for example has argued as follows: all the children in a certain clinic come from the same ethnic group (Italian, let us say), but the ones from middle-class homes are brighter than those from working-class homes. Since they all come from the same gene pool, the difference between them must be of environmental origin, due to the kind of homes they are reared in. This is absurd. It begs the question by assuming what the authors set out to prove, namely that all members of an ethnic group have the same genetic endowment, and does not even consider the logical alternative that middle-class homes are middle-class because the parents have superior genetic endowments that they also pass on to the children. The argument has no significance at all.

Another critic denies that the IQ measures something that determines how well a child will do in school. When social level is held constant the IQ has little predictive value, so social level is the true determinant of success in school. This argument too has a large hole in it. It overlooks the possibility that the IQ, determining the levels of school success in preceding generations, is in effect a main determinant of social level. The argument could as well have gone like this: Holding IQ constant, social level is a poor predictor of school success, so it is the IQ that is the real determinant, not social level. Or try this analogy: I have a theory that age is a determinant of weight in the growing child. I determine the correlation of age and weight between the ages of 2 and 12, and it is high, which supports my theory. You however object, saying that height is an important variable, so you recalculate the correlation holding height constant. You find that age has little effect in children of the same height—so age is not a factor in a child's weight, it is all due to his height.

It is evidently still difficult to think logically in the heredity-environment business.

6 A Physiological Theory

The theory of cell-assemblies is a theory of thought and a general theory of behavior, but it began at a more modest level. My problem was to understand some of the effects of brain operation, and in particular how it was that a patient might have a large chunk of brain tissue removed without much effect on his IQ or his intelligence as it seemed to his family. How could there be no loss of intelligence after surgical removal of both prefrontal lobes (about a sixth of the mass of the cerebrum) or removal of the entire right half of the cortex? The only answer seemed to be that intelligence, as measured, somehow concerned the kind of concepts the patient had developed while growing up and the way he had learned to think about the common situations of everyday life, and that these ways of thinking, once established, were not easily changed. But such an answer only moved the problem over into another area. What is a concept? How is a way of thinking established, and why should it last?

There are complications here that still must be reckoned with by anyone who would really explain human behavior. In particular, there is a crucial difficulty in reconciling the theory of learning with the theory of perception, and it seems to be avoided both by the learning theorist and the perceptionist. ("Learning theorists," self-named, have in common a narrow view of learning that derives ultimately from Watson's stimulus-response proposals and his denial of mental processes; and I coin the term *perceptionist* to refer similarly to one with a narrow view of perception, without regard to the problems of learning.) In both cases a black-box approach is taken, which permits one to avoid the constraints originating in the structure of the brain. Much can be done, and is done, with such nonphysiological theory, but the theory must ultimately be translatable into or concordant with the language of the anatomist and the physiologist. Physiology is not the whole answer by any means, but "physiologizing" may at times reveal difficulty that would otherwise remain unsuspected (p. 42).

Showing how the theory of cell-assemblies was developed is one way to show what the difficulties are, or some of them, and perhaps is the clearest way to explicate the theory itself. This also has some interest as an example of theorizing in the real world, with its doubts and difficulties and false starts, unlike the idealized and simplified cases to be found in the textbooks of logic. Logicians prefer to discuss cases of outright success (good theory) or outright failure (bad theory). It is surely of some interest to see how an author could get himself into the position of having to publish a theory of perception that he actively disbelieved, but published nevertheless because it was a necessary part of a larger theoretical scheme that did have value (and eventually got independent support). But the experiments that showed that the theory was right—more or less—also showed that it was wrong: a situation that will be clear later in this chapter. It appears that the theory was, and is, on the right track or aimed in the right general direction, but still has a long way to go.

The theory is physiological in the sense only that is uses the available physiological evidence and attempts to say in physiologically intelligible terms what kind of activity goes on in the brain. But it is still theory, and it is important to make clear that the problem must be dealt with theoretically; and that this is a *psychological* problem. There is no possibility whatever of solving the problem of the over-all patterns of activity in the brain by physiological methods. There is no possibility for example of putting in enough electrodes to record the patterns of neural firing in thought. Ten thousand electrodes could not do the trick. Thought must be known as theoretically as the chemist knows the atom. Physiological methods can deal with part systems: for example, with input from retina to striate and peristriate cortex or output from Betz cells to spinal cord and thence to muscle; with the effects of damage to the red nucleus or the behavioral effects of removing the amygdala; and so on. All such information is fundamental, but a further fundamental feature is missing, namely, how these part systems are coordinated in the ordinary behavior of the intact unanesthetized animal. We know much of how visual excitations reach the cortex, of how the motor cortex interacts with cerebellum and the nuclei of the midbrain to control spinal cord activity and thereby the activity of the muscles, but there is no physiological account available of how Hubel and Wiesel's visual edge detectors determine motor output when a cat's eye is caught by a mouse running across the floor. There is no prospect of getting such an account, or of learning by physiological means what goes on in the cortex when human eyes are engaged in reading a novel.

If present theoretical answers to such questions are poor, it is nevertheless only by means of developing better theory that we can hope for better answers. Understanding the integrative action of the whole brain is a psychoneurological or a neuropsychological problem, a highly theoretical enterprise that depends on bringing together the results of anatomical, physiological and behavioral analysis. That is what the theory of cell-assemblies tries to do.

THE PROBLEM OF PERCEPTION

The facts of perception represent the first great hurdle for theory, now as in 1945 (when cell-assemblies were first thought of, especially to deal with this problem). A conflict with the theory of learning is due to the apparent fact that the perception does not, or need not, depend on the excitation of any particular input lines, and hence the apparent necessity of concluding that a perceptual process is not localized—may not have to be an activity of any particular cells in the brain. But learning must depend on changes in particular cells; and any response to perception must be in particular muscles and so must be determined by particular motor pathways from brain to cord to muscles. If the locus of a perceptual activity is variable, if it is now an activity of one set of neurons, now of another, how can a perception be affected by learning, and how can it excite the proper output path and not a lot of other paths?

Learning is a changed pattern of conduction in the brain that results from experience and makes a change of response potential. In the simplest case (the formation of an S-R connection) excitation from the stimulus reaches a muscle or gland that it did not reach before, making a new response. In the more complex case of cognitive learning there is often no response at the time the learning occurs; a new ideational system is organized or a connection is made between two such systems, for example, and it is only later when, in the right circumstances, some change of response shows that the learning did occur. If this changed pattern of conduction persists it is memory; and the persistence, it seems clear, means that the learning must be a change related to particular pathways, or particular neurons. In other words it must be a localized effect.

But this seems not to be true of perception, which—appparently—may be excited by different sets of input lines every time it occurs and so cannot be localized. So it seems, at least with familiar objects. A book or a cow or a car is recognized not only in different parts of the visual field—you don't have to look right at one of them to perceive it—but also when it is seen from different angles and at different distances. Lashley and Köhler both believed in fact that what matters in perception is not what sensory receptors are stimulated but only the *Gestalt*, the form or pattern of stimulation. However, no one was able to show how learning could take place with repeated trials, if the input never followed the same input lines and the same central pathways. The effect of a second trial cannot sum with the effect of the first if they are in different places in the brain. And this Gestalt-Lashleyan theory never succeeded in showing how a perception can excite a specific response. When a learned response is made to a perception, at *some* point the excitation from the stimulating event must get on a specific set of motor pathways to produce that response.

Köhler never faced the problem (at least not in his published work). Lashley recognized it and tried to deal with it by his theory of interference patterns, but concluded that the theory was unsuccessful (he was given to saying that he had destroyed all theories of behavior, including his own).

A related modern idea is the hologram, which it seems likely Lashley could not have approved any more than his own interference patterns. By analogy with the optical hologram of the physical scientist, the brain hologram is supposed to be widely dispersed but to contain all the information in each of its parts; thus it does not matter where a perceived object is in the visual field, or by which fibers in the optic nerve the information is transmitted. But essential difficulties remain. First, different perceptions result from the same sensory input, though the hologram must be the same. Figure 9 is the classic example, from Edgar Rubin, the Danish psychologist. Without eye movement, so that the sensory input remains the same, one sees at one moment a vase or goblet, at another moment two faces in profile staring at one another. This variability of perception is not limited to such ambiguous figures—they serve only to provide clearcut examples—but is universal. Depending on what is going on in your thought at the time, when you look at a chair what you may perceive is its size, its color, a distinctive feature of its shape, its distance from the table—or all these and other features one after another in close succession. The difficulty for hologram theory is to account

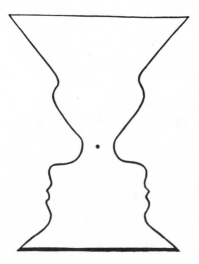

FIG. 9.   The ambiguous or reversible figure. With gaze fixed on the center dot one can perceive either goblet or profiles, so eye movement is not necessary to the change from one percept to the other. After Rubin, from Hebb (1972). By permission.

for this influence of one's attitude (essentially, one's preexistent mental activity) upon what is perceived, and the resulting variability of perception. Another difficulty is the constancy of the visual world, and the fact that the other end of the room does not look different as your eyes move, or when you move from one point to another, although the brain hologram is modified with each such movement.

An answer that has been suggested for such criticism is to say that the hologram is not the percept but gives rise to it. In that case the theory is of no help, and in fact is not a theory of perception at all, until we know what the activity is that it gives rise to and how it does so. The original idea was ingenious and attractive, but the attraction is superficial until we see how to deal with the ambiguous figure and the variability of the percept despite an unchanging sensory input; with the selectivity of attention and the influence of the immediately preceding cerebral activity; and with the fact that the process of perception is characteristically sequential and not like a single photographic recording, except possibly with highly familiar objects. There are other difficulties—visual completions, subjective contours, perceptual learning—and until some at least of these are dealt with the hologram remains at the level of analogy.

As an alternative, cell-assembly theory has the disadvantage of awkwardness. It makes of the simplest perceptions a complexity that seems far from the directness and *ease* of the perception of a familiar voice or the sight of a familiar object. Students of perception have traditionally inclined toward nativism, and any theory is unpalatable that makes the ease of perception of common objects the result of a long process of learning. They have also inclined toward denying that the perception of the whole depends on perception of parts, and thus assembly theory is at best unattractive because, although it does not reduce the whole to a sum of sensory elements, it does argue that any but the simplest of objects is first perceived (in the course of the child's development) as consisting of parts, the whole being perceived as such only later. The theory has experimental support, and it is possible that human perception actually does have the kind of complexity that the theory requires, but it certainly looked improbable to its author—me—when it was first conceived.

DEVISING AN IMPROBABLE THEORY

The problem of perception remained intractable for about five years (1939 to 1944) and as a result I made no progress in my attempt to understand concepts and thought. It seemed obvious that concepts, like images, must derive from perception, and I could think of no mechanism of perception that corresponded to my ("perceptionist") preconceptions. In fact, by 1944 I had given up trying to solve the problem. What happened then was that I became aware of some recent work of Lorente de Nó in conjunction with some observations of Hilgard and Marquis (1940), which led me to think of a possible solution for a different problem: the problem of set and attention. And this brought me straight back to concepts and the thought process, but now from a different point of view.

In 1940, set, in various manifestations and known by various names such as attention, intention, attitude, expectancy, and so forth, constituted an entirely unsolved problem. As Gibson (1941) showed, the effect, whatever produced it, was ubiquitous in psychological investigation, freely recognized by the cognitivist but also by some hard-line experimentalists who would rather not; on the other hand, not even a suggested mechanism was available by way of explanation. Attention and set were a mystery, until Hilgard and Marquis's references to an activity of the brain that is relatively free from sensory control showed where the trouble must lie: in that through-transmission nervous system represented in Figure 10, with a brain that can do nothing but act as errand boy in the delivery of sensory messages to the muscles. Set was a mystery because it meant that the brain was doing something that—it seemed—the brain could not do; but if on the contrary the brain can act independently of the sense organs, then set and attention and attitude could be understood.

Figure 10 diagrams two kinds of transmission in the nervous system. One is built in, one acquired. The first is the basis of the unconditioned reflex, a

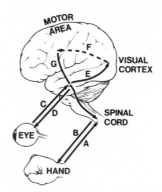

FIG. 10.   Fact and fantasy combined: reflex and learning. The solid lines A, B, C, D, E and G schematically represent built-in reflex connections, A-B for the clasp reflex of the newborn (stimulate the palm and the fingers close), C-D for the pupillary contraction in bright light. E represents the pathway by which visual stimulation reaches the cortex, and G the pyramidal tract from the motor cortex to the spinal cord. Surgical stimulation of the latter path will make a patient's hand move whether he wants to or not. All these effects are automatic. The broken line F is a theoretical idea of an earlier day, concerning learning: the idea that visual cortex gets a new connection direct to motor cortex whenever a visual stimulus is conditioned to arouse a motor response (as diagramed, a movement of the hand). But such a connection is now known to be fantasy only.

function of the spinal cord or brain stem (the stem is the extension of the cord into the skull), but not of the cortex. The representation is schematic, but sound enough in principle. The second is a longer route, from sense organ to cortex, to another point in the cortex, and thence to the spinal cord and out to the musculature. Like the first pathway, it is a straight-through sensorimotor connection; unlike the first, it has no basis in reality, as far as the crucial link F is concerned. This was supposed to be formed in the course of learning, and Lashley (1930, 1950) showed that such direct connections do not exist.

The essential basis of an alternative view was provided by Lorente de Nó, who showed that the cortex is throughout its extent largely composed of enormously complex closed or re-entrant paths, rather than linear connections only between more distant points. A small sample appears in Figure 11. A cortex so organized offers a very different theoretical situation.

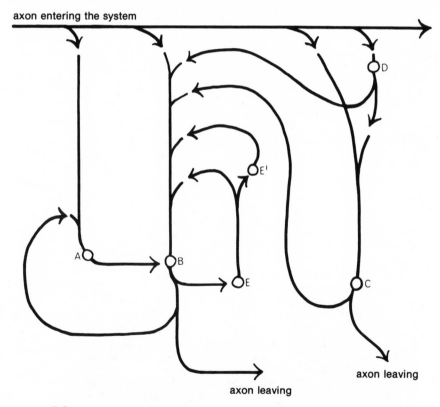

axon entering the system

axon leaving

axon leaving

FIG. 11   Reverberatory circuits in the cortex. A single fiber from outside the system excites four neurons, A, B, C, D. A excites B, which re-excites A as well as exciting E. E re-excites B directly and also indirectly via E^1, and so on. Two of the four neurons send their axons out of the system, so that the internal activity will have effects elsewhere. Based on a drawing by Lorente de Nó. From Hebb (1972). By permission.

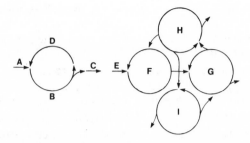

FIG. 12.   Schematizing the closed circuits by which the brain can hold an excitation and maintain its own internal activity. *Left*, the simplest case: a pathway A excites reverberation B-D-B-D-..., which permits a single volley from A to result in prolonged firing by C. *Right*, interaction of self-re-exciting systems ("cell-assemblies"), with reverberation of reverberations.

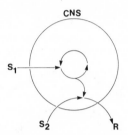

FIG. 13.   Schematizing the mechanism of set. The first of two stimuli, S_1, excites a central activity, which by itself is not sufficient to determine the response but maintains its activity until S_2 is presented, exciting an immediate response R.

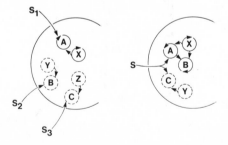

FIG. 14.   The mechanism of selective attention. *Left*, S_1, S_2 and S_3 are sensory stimulations tending to excite central processes A, B, and C respectively; a prior activity X (something thought about) is connected with A and so S_1 and X can reinforce one another's effect. Thus S_1 arouses percept A. But Y and Z, central processes connected with B and C, are inactive, provide no support, so S_2 and S_3 fail to have any effect (do not enter consciousness). *Right*, the same sensory event can arouse different perceptions (e.g., at sunrise, one may perceive the sun moving upwards or the earth rolling downwards). In the diagram, stimulation coincides with a central activity X; with that support, S excites the percept or thought process A-B. If Y had been active instead of X, S would have excited C, a different percept.

When an excitation reaches the cortex, instead of having to be transmitted at once to a motor path, or else die out, it may travel round and round in these closed paths and may continue to do so after the original sensory stimulation has ceased. This is schematized in Figure 12. A delayed response to stimulation is now possible and, fundamentally, a mechanism of thought now becomes intelligible, as a complex activity entirely within the brain in which one closed system excites another, that one exciting a third or re-exciting the first, and so on. These central processes of course continue to receive sensory inputs also; most of the time thought processes are in touch with the sensory environment and are influenced by it.

Set and attention then become intelligible also. In the clearest case, set occurs when two stimuli are presented one after the other and the response to the second is controlled or modified by the first. The first "sets" the subject to respond to the second. In the hundred yards' dash, the *ready* signal prepares the runner for the *go* and produces a faster start. In the Würzburg experiment referred to in Chapter 2 (p. 19), the instruction to the subject to add (or subtract) is the first stimulus, the presentation of digits such as 6 and 2 is the second; the response "eight" (or with the other set, "four") is obviously determined by both stimuli, not by the second alone. The effect of the first must be held till the second is presented. The nervous system of Figure 10 had no way of holding, and so set was a mystery. Figures 13 and 14 show how the existence of holding mechanisms in the brain removes the mystery from both set and attention.

Another mystery was banished at the same time. In 1939, Brogden (1939) showed that dogs were capable of associating two sensory events. This too was impossible for the nervous system of Figure 10, which is designed to permit sensorimotor associations, but not sensory-sensory ones (see also Fig. 6, p.34). Brogden exposed the dog to a light and a sound simultaneously; he then conditioned the light to a response, and having done so tested the dog with the sound—and obtained the same response, though the sound and the response had not been paired. I have already pointed out, in an earlier discussion (p. 35), that although the learning theorists had forsworn any interest in the nervous system, they continued in effect to deny the existence of any psychological phenomenon that was inconsistent with the nervous system as it was known to Watson in 1920. Brogden's results could not be denied, but for twenty years or more there were persistent attempts at explaining them away—although by now it had become easy to see how the central representative processes could become associated, if the two stimuli excited activity in reverberatory closed pathways and not mere straight-through transmissions.

I need hardly say that such ideas were very interesting, with their suggestion of solutions for long-standing problems of behavior. But serious difficulties showed up at once, including my old difficulty with perception, and I did not feel that I had made a "discovery," or that the problems were really solved.

However, the ideas *were* attractive, and I worked with them as a sort of game, to see how far the difficulties might be reduced.

The first point was that one of these self-re-exciting systems could not consist of one circuit of two or three neurons, but must have a number of circuits, both because of "subnormality" or fatigue (when one circuit fatigues temporarily another can continue) and to be able to deliver a sufficiently massive excitation to another such system to fire it. I could assume that when a number of neurons in the cortex are excited by a given sensory input they tend to become interconnected, some of them at least forming a multicircuit closed system. Eventually such a system was called a cell-assembly, so that term can be used here. The idea then was that a *percept* consists of assemblies excited sensorily, a *concept* of assemblies excited centrally, by other assemblies.

And this brought me back to the problem of the localization of a percept. The fundamental idea of the theory as it was later published (Hebb, 1949) was that repeated exposure to a given sensory stimulation will organize an assembly, and the difficulty I have already referred to now became inescapable. A familiar object is recognizable at different distances, at different angles, and in different parts of the visual field—left, right, above or below the direction of vision. In each case, the retinal stimulation is different and so a different cortical excitation results. In each case, it seemed, a separate assembly would be required, amounting to a large number for each recognizable object and meaning that visual recognition would have to be separately learned for each direction, distance, and aspect of the object as seen. An improbable conclusion, to say the least. Regretfully, I saw that the idea would not work. It was too interesting to give up entirely, but I could not take it seriously.

The game then was to see whether the general idea could be made less improbable. For one thing, suppose that it is not the whole object that one must learn to see separately in its different aspects but the component parts. The fundamental work on perception in animals had been done with simple figures such as square and triangle, so I asked what the effect would be of supposing that what one learns to perceive is not a triangle as a whole but the three angles or the three sides.

At once there was a simplification of the problem. A large triangle and a small triangle of similar shape have identical parts as far as foveal (central) vision is concerned, as Figure 15 shows. The same thing applies when the same triangle is seen at different distances, so it would not be necessary in the first place to have to learn separately to recognize it for each size and each distance. And here I made a small discovery. In playing the game I was looking at the experimental data from a new point of view and I suddenly realized that the whole literature was biased by the tacit assumption that eye movement is unimportant in visual perception (except, of course, when fine

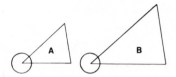

FIG. 15. Identity of part-perceptions. The small and large triangles, as wholes, cannot excite the same retinal cells at the same time but with separate fixations can have a series of identical effects in central vision (represented by the circles).

detail must be examined closely). Now it is true that the tachistoscope, which presents the visual object for too short a time to permit eye movement, shows that perception of a familiar object is possible without looking at its parts one after another, but this is not true of strange objects. It cannot be true when visual perception is first developing; for the newborn, all visual objects are strange. Even with things as apparently simple as a triangle the infant may have to fixate the three angles repeatedly, one after another, before ever managing to perceive the triangle as a whole. (Arbitrarily, in 1945, I picked the angles to theorize about; 15 years later, in the stabilized-image experiments described in the next chapter, it appeared that the three sides would have been a better guess.)

It was a surprise to see how much the problem was changed by taking account of eye movement and a variable fixation. The cell-assembly notion began to look less absurd. But this was still a game. It still implied that a baby must slowly learn even to *see* the world, quite apart from learning what things mean or how they behave: I thought, a most unlikely idea. It implied too that an adult would not perceive strange objects when not even their parts were familiar: still more unlikely. However, I had just discovered how biased my notions were concerning eye movement. Maybe my biases were still showing. Was there any way to look at the question experimentally?

Could one devise a completely strange environment in which to test an animal's perceptions? Easy enough to prepare one in which there are no familiar objects, but any livable environment must be made up of much of the same set of perceptual elements: in the visual sphere, contours of variable slope, various colors both darker and lighter, curved and plane surfaces and their intersections; noises of various pitch, complexity, intensity and temporal pattern; roughness, sharpness or roundedness of edges and points, vibrations, and so on: These are components of which any environment is made up and must be familiar, strange as the combinations in which they occur may happen to be.

As I thought about this aspect of the question, the special case of vision came to mind. It *is* possible to rear an animal in darkness and at maturity expose him to an environment that in one respect at least is totally strange.

Nine years earlier in fact I had reared rats in darkenss myself and tested their vision, as the basis of a Ph.D. thesis. When I recalled that work I recalled too a feeling that there was something peculiar, something remarkable, about a book I had read at the time. The book was von Senden's (1932, 1960) valuable compilation of all the published case reports of people who were born blind, with cataract, and who were later made able to see by removing the cataract. I looked at von Senden again and was astonished at what I found.[10] His subjects were in effect blind at first, as the game I was playing suggested. They could distinguish and respond to colors but had practically no perception of shape or pattern. (All that was "peculiar" about these reports, earlier, was that they flatly contradicted my beliefs.) A prolonged learning process was needed after operation before the patient began to see the world in the way that a normal person does. The learning was so arduous that most of the patients eventually gave up the attempt and returned to living as blind persons.

Now my attitude had to change. What I had thought too unlikely to be considered looked as though it was true, and the game had to become a serious investigation. The change was reinforced when Austin Riesen, entirely by coincidence, chose that time to bring out into the light two young chimpanzees who had been in darkness from birth (Riesen, 1947). We were both working in the Yerkes Laboratories of Primate Biology and the baby chimpanzees had been reared in darkness with the general expectation that perception would be unimpaired by the lack of visual stimulation. They showed exactly the opposite, and to a degree that was astonishing to us all— me least perhaps, because I had been rereading von Senden, but I was astonished too. For the two animals showed no sign of awareness of the new stimulation to which they were exposed in the normally lighted laboratory. Von Senden's human patients were verbally prepared for what was to happen. They were immediately responsive when the bandages were removed from their eyes, could perceive that something was there when an object was held in front of them, and could even tell sometimes that a circle and a square were in

---

[10]My failure to see the apparent meaning of von Senden's evidence is a perfect example of how theory, firmly entrenched, can block one's vision. My thesis research was done under the influence of holistic and more or less nativistic ideas—with the result that I did not see the implication even of my own data. My experiments had shown no difference in the perception of brightness and size by normal and dark-reared rats. At that time no one suggested that the perception of patterns might be different, so I thought I had settled the question: perception is normal in the absence of prior experience. I went on to look at pattern perception and found that the perception, once established, is about the same in normal and dark-reared—patterns that look alike to one look alike to the other—but failed totally to reflect on the fact that establishing the perception took six times as long in the dark-reared. Only when I came back to my own published data, nine years later and with light from another theoretical idea, did I see what I had done. Fortunately no one else had seen either: The Gestalt-minded knew I was right, the neo-Watsonian knew I was wrong (and working with a nonproblem as well), so neither felt any need to look at the supporting data.

some way different. There was no sign of this in the chimpanzees. Visual reflexes were strongly marked, but there was not the slightest suggestion of any other response. There was no effect of the visual stimulation on the behavior of the whole animal. There was no attempt to explore visual objects tactually, and no evidence of any emotional reaction to this completely strange experience.

The two young animals, I thought, had formed no visual cell-assemblies whose activity would be perception and which would have permitted thought about the new phenomena and an investigation of them. My scheme had suggested that the genuinely unfamiliar could not be perceived or thought about and now it seemed that I had confirmation, full and running over.

It is entirely fitting, in this story of stumbling discovery, to report that the evidence that converted me to belief, without which I might well have dropped the whole thing, was later shown to be bad. It was certainly not the crucial evidence that it seemed. The two young chimpanzees were not merely facing a strange environment, they were facing it with defective equipment. Chow, Riesen and Newell (1957) eventually found that rearing in darkness causes the death of some of the cells in the chimpanzee's retina (although not in the rat's: K.S. Lashley, interested in the structural basis of rat vision, examined the eyes of the rats I had reared in darkness and found no degeneration). Again, the eye of a kitten covered with translucent plastic, and thus deprived of patterned stimulation during growth, loses some of its central connections (Hubel & Wiesel, 1963). Either or both of these defects may have been present in von Senden's patients. At the time however I had no suspicion that this was so: There were those who thought than an unstimulated cell might eventually die, in what was called "trans-synaptic degeneration," but their views at the time were not widely accepted in physiology. Thinking that the case for the theory of cell-assemblies was now established, I set out in earnest to see what its other implications were.

There were of course still difficulties. The next one unexpectedly widened the enquiry to take in the topic of emotion.

Here I was still concerned with the problem of strangeness. At the earlier stage I might have rejected the ideas with which I was working because they meant that a truly strange object could not be perceived—and then Riesen's evidence and von Senden's showed me that this might really be true, peculiar as it seemed. Now the question concerned the effect of strangeness on the stream of thought. If thought is a series of cell-assembly activities, these must ordinarily be excited both sensorily and centrally. When event A in the familiar environment has always been followed by event B, as perceived, the corresponding cell-assembly a will have been regularly followed by assembly b, and therefore will have connections with it and tend to excite it; or if A instead has been followed at various times by one or other of a set of events C, D, or E, a, instead of exciting b strongly, will excite c, d, and e somewhat less

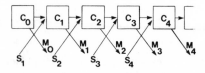

FIG. 16. Relating sensory input (S) to central processes (C) and motor outflow (M). C_1 to C_4 represent the whole activity of the brain at four successive moments in time. At any moment that central activity is determined *both* by the immediately preceding activity and by sensory input; motor response follows. Obviously the response is not determined by sensation alone. See also Figure 17.

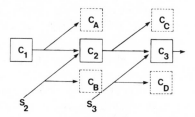

FIG. 17. The relation between sensation and thought (between S and C in Figure 16). C, central process; S, sensory input. C_1 might give rise to various sequels; these are represented by C_A and C_2. S_2 also tends to excite different central activities; these are represented by C_2 and C_B. Both excite C_2, which therefore is the upshot. What is not shown is the possibility that a strongly established central activity might take off without sensory support, as in daydreaming; or the possibility that a sudden sensory input, unrelated to the current central activity, might break it up, the effect being startle.

strongly. The situation is diagrammed in Figures 16 and 17. In this scheme, the facilitation from *a* is the basis of expectancy. It is implied that there is a certain correspondence between expectancy and what is then perceived. That proposition was quite acceptable, but it had a corollary. In a strange environment, thought ought to be disrupted, or might be disrupted, by the lack of correspondence between central facilitation and sensory input. In short, thought might be disorganized in a really strange environment.

Here, "strange environment" does not merely mean a place where one has never been before, but one in which the ordinary concordances are absent. It must not be too strange, for it was implied that the problem would arise when things were perceived—but perceived in the wrong relation to each other. Again it seemed that the theory was pointing in the wrong direction. One might have trouble adjusting to such an environment but surely one would still be able to think.

Once more, the chimpanzee to the rescue. In the preceding months my experimental work (as distinct from playing theoretical games) had been a study of personality and emotion in the animals of the Yerkes colony. I had stumbled on the fear aroused by a model of a chimpanzee head (p. 60) and related objects, and was completely puzzled by it. The phenomena were obviously significant and must be reported, if only as a reminder of the human reaction to sight of a major operation or to contact with a dead body: a reaction that is persistently avoided or forgotten in the psychological textbooks. I prepared a report of the facts with no attempt at explanation. The paper was ready for dispatch to the *Psychological Review* when suddenly I realized what it was describing: a series of situations in which strangeness, a departure from day-to-day experience, was disruptive of behavior (and presumably of thought). The strange situations—a head lacking a body, a model that looked like an animal but obviously was not, the inert body of a chimpanzee being freely handled by the human staff—were not quite what I had been thinking of, and the disruption of behavior was not what I had thought of either: but disruption there was, and plain to be seen.

Now I had a theoretical explanation: Emotion is a disruption of cell-assemblies. The explanation had gaps and minor inconsistencies, but it needed only a slight extension to offer, in general terms, a rational and comprehensive account of fear and its near relatives anger, shyness, and depression. Nothing of the kind existed in the literature. Another bonus was that it drew attention to the extent of the phenomena of emotional disturbance, of which the literature at the time gave no hint.

The theoretical account turned out to be grossly incomplete, since I knew nothing at the time of the arousal system nor of the limbic system, both of which are intimately concerned in emotion. It may be that the disruption of cell-assembly activity is only a precipitant of emotional disturbance instead of being itself the emotion, but this theory still offers the only relatively complete account of the conditions giving rise to fear, anger, and so on, and the only suggestion about what they have in common. In addition to the conflict between expectancy (including desire) and what one perceives, the simple absence of accustomed sensory input might disrupt cell-assemblies that are excited centrally but are dependent also on sensory excitation for stable functioning. This would account for a number of "deficit reactions," such as the three-year-old's fear of the dark and the depression of loneliness or homesickness in older subjects. Finally, malnutrition and endocrine change could disrupt, a changed blood chemistry disturbing time relations in the assembly. Here would be comprised the neurotic reactions of U.S. servicemen in the second World War who did not eat enough salt to compensate for heavy sweating in the tropics, the psychotic fears described in cases of pellagra (lack of B-complex), and the depression of the menstrual cycle. None of these conclusions could be rigorously deduced from the theory, but they were possible inferences, and they introduced order into a topic where no order existed previously. At this point the theory seemed to be ready for launching.

I published a preliminary report (Hebb, 1946), began the preparation of a more complete account, and started the experimentation that the theory called for.

EXPERIMENTAL TESTS:
THE EARLY ENVIRONMENT

The main validation of the theory was found in three sets of experiments. It is fine to have found a rationale for set and attention and to discover how the varied phenomena of emotional disturbance might be fitted into an organized theoretical scheme, but the case for the actual existence of cell-assemblies became much more firm with the support of new experimental data. The first of the three investigations concerned the effects of the early environment on intelligence and thought, the second, its effects at maturity, and these two are discussed here. The third, which concerned perception, will be left till the following chapter.

The theory proposed that thought processes (and therefore the operations of intelligence) consist of an activity of cell-assemblies, and that these assemblies are organized in the first place by sensory stimulation from the young animal's normal environment. The first experiment therefore was a test to see if animals that had had a good environment during growth would be better problem-solvers at maturity than ones from a poor environment.

A preliminary test was made with two litters of pet rats, compared to cage-reared littermates. From the point of view of the theory, rearing in the small laboratory cages must fall short of an adequate perceptual stimulation; the pet rats on the other hand, taken home to be reared by my two young daughters and having the run of the house much of the time, had a much wider exposure and should be more intelligent. At maturity both the laboratory group and the pets were tested with a rat-intelligence test that had been developed by Kenneth Williams (Hebb & Williams, 1946) and later improved by Rabinovitch and Rosvold (1952). The results of this preliminary work looked good and a more formal investigation was set up by Bernard Hymovitch. He devised for some rats a radically restricted environment (but with all the comforts of home, apart from boredom) and an enriched or "free" environment for others, in a large wooden cage containing a number of objects to make what he called a Coney Island for rats. The principal results agreed with the theory: The rats reared in restriction were greatly inferior to the free-environment rats.

But two further results were of almost equal interest. Hymovitch also showed that the environmental effect occurs only during the period of growth. One group of rats, reared in restriction, were put for an equal period of time into the free environment, as adults; another, reared in the free environment, were restricted as adults. Both were then tested and the second group were much better than the first. In other words, the effect of the early environment on intelligence was not reversible. This closely parallels the human data. The environmental influence on the IQ is limited essentially to the period of growth, ending somewhere between the ages of 12 and 18.[11] A favorable environment thereafter cannot reverse the damage that has been produced by an unfavorable environment earlier.

The other extra in Hymovitch's experiments was a demonstration of the extent of visual-perceptual learning that the rat is capable of. One group of animals was reared in small wire-mesh cages that let their occupants see the outside world but permitted no locomotion. The rat could turn around and stand up or lie down, no more. The cages were placed in daily rotation in a series of places in the experimental room and in the free-environment cage so as to give the animals an extensive visual experience of the environment but no experience whatever of exploring it. The wholly surprising result was that these animals were as good in solving maze problems as the free-environment group (which could explore but did not have as wide a visual experience) and of course much better than the restricted. Skeptical of this result, Forgays and Forgays (1952) repeated the experiment and showed that the mesh-cage group were not quite as good as the free-environment group, but still confirmed Hymovitch's results of extensive benefit from a purely visual experience.

The dog is nearer man in psychological complexity. If the results of the rat experiments were to be relevant for man it was of value to see if the same results would be obtained with the higher animal. Thompson and Heron (1954) and Melzack and Scott (1957) reared Scottish terriers in two ways: in restriction, and with the degree of freedom that a pet dog usually has. The restricted dogs during the whole period of growth were in small single cages where they could hear and smell other dogs and the human occupants of the lab, but could not see or touch or be touched by them. Whereas an adult dog would be miserable in such circumstances, being used to more freedom, these dogs knew nothing else and in the words of an experienced dog handler were happy as larks. Their littermates were given as pets to members of the university community and their friends, with the understanding that they would be recalled on occasion for testing in the laboratory.

The effects of restriction were more extreme than in the rat experiment. Thompson and Heron showed that the restricted dogs were inferior to the pet

---

[11]Fifteen years is usually taken as the age at which intelligence, as measured by intelligence tests, stops growing, but there is reason to think that the development may stop earlier with low IQs and continue longer with high ones. Weisenberg, Roe and McBride's (1936) unique sample of U.S. adults and U.S. Army data of 1918 (Yerkes, 1921) both suggest that the average is about 13. That would mean that the limit of development varies from perhaps 11 years for the low IQ to 18 or 19 for the high IQ.

group in the solution of maze problems and in a number of insight tests devised especially for the investigation. They were untrainable, abnormal in personality and social behavior in ways that were hard to describe ("I never saw a dog like that before"), and could not be bred, though physically they were splendid animals.

Melzack and Scott's research dealt with the most striking peculiarity of all. The dogs reared in restriction were unmindful of pain. The reflex response was normal but the emotional or motivational component was missing. It may be recalled that after lobotomy, for intractable pain, the human patient may say that the pain is the same—but doesn't bother him any longer (p. 5). Thus pain must have two components, a recognizable sensory quality and, for normally reared dogs and normal proplem, an accompanying strong emotional reaction. The restricted dogs acted as if lobotomized. One of them saw a lighted cigar fall on the floor and thrust his nose into the flowing coal to investigate it. He pulled back reflexively, but touched the coal with his nose twice more. In experimental tests, electric shock elicited the same reflexive withdrawal, but produced no subsequent avoidance of the electrically charged object.

Clearly, the motivational and emotional qualities of pain stimuli are a function of a normal infant experience.

THE ADULT ENVIRONMENT

The animal experiments showed in brief that the normal growth of the mind requires the sensory stimulation of the normal complex environment. The next study, using human subjects, showed that the integrity of the mind at maturity continues to depend on that stimulation. This was the so-called sensory-deprivation experiment—which, since it did not deprive the subject of sensory stimulation but did prevent perception, might better be thought of as a perceptual-deprivation or perceptual-isolation experiment.

The experiment was done by Woodburn Heron and collaborators, W.R. Bexton, B.K. Doane, and T.H. Scott (Heron, 1957). They hired college students to do nothing—or very little, such as answering a few questions at testing time—for 24 hours a day. The subjects were well paid to lie quietly on a comfotable bed; wore translucent but not transparent goggles; heard a constant slight buzzing sound from a small speaker in the foam-rubber pillow except when the experimenter was on the line with a test question; and wore long cardboard cuffs from the middle of the forearm to beyond the fingers. Thus they received much sensory stimulation, but all of it unpatterned except in the tests or occasional requests for information. Excepted also are the breaks in which the subject ate or went to the toilet, although he wore the goggles over his eyes throughout. It was estimated that on the average 22 hours a day were spent in full restriction.

The main results: The subject's ability to solve problems "in his head"— mental arithmetic problems, anagrams and the like that could be attempted while in restriction—declined from about the end of the first day onward, and coherent thought became harder to maintain. Some of the subjects entered the experiment with the intention of planning future work or reviewing mentally for examinations. The reports were consistent that this soon became impossible, and there were even complaints that it was hard or impossible to daydream. Beginning about the third day there were increasingly complex visual hallucinations as well as a few somesthetic ones (referred to earlier: p. 26). For some hours after emerging from the experiment, visual perception was also greatly disturbed. The experimental subjects were more vulnerable to propaganda than the control subjects who were hired to listen to the same stuff, advocating belief in ghosts and poltergeists as well as clairvoyance and telepathy. (The message was that scientists who don't believe in ghosts or ESP are biased and refuse to consider the evidence; both groups were affected by it, but the experimental subjects much more.) And finally, the experimental subjects showed a 10% slowing of the EEG, a most surprising result, demonstrating a physiological change of brain function as a result of a mere lack of pattern in the input from the sense organs.

As far as theoretical predictions are concerned, the prediction that intelligence would be impaired by restriction in infancy was reasonably specific and was confirmed. The personality change in dogs was not predicted, nor the relative insensitivity to pain, but these results strengthen the more general proposition, quite consistent with the theory, that the early environment has a vital organizing function in mental activity at maturity. Similarly, the specific results of the perceptual-isolation experiment were not predictable, but their general tenor supported the prediction that *was* made, that such conditions would have a disorganizing effect on thought.

But it is important to say also that in some respects the theory was contradicted by the results. The students who entered the isolation experiment showed no impairment of problem-solving ability for some 24 hours, and other abnormalities appeared even later. The theory has no way yet of accounting for that delay. Similarly, the subjects showed a good deal of unanimity in reporting after isolation that it took 24 to 36 hours to recover motivation and to resume normal work patterns. Together with the results of the stabilized-image work reported in the following chapter, these experiments show that the theory is of the right kind but has far to go. The experiments with stabilized images reported in the next chapter show, I think conclusively, that cell-assemblies exist, but the isolation experiment described here shows that there is much that we do not understand about how they function.

7

Perception and Cognitive Development

I have already referred to the classical conflict between ideas about perception and ideas about learning. It seemed that a perceptual process could have no specific locus in the brain; but perception is a source of learning and establishes memories, and for this reason, it seemed, *must* be localized. Also, perception gives rise to specific responses and so must transmit excitations to specific efferent pathways. It seemed therefore that some way had to be found to localize the perceptual process, theoretically, and this necessity was a main determinant of the proposed characteristics of a cell-assembly. I have also said that the result was distasteful and violated my pre-existing ideas about perception, although I could find no conclusive evidence to oppose the new theory or support the pre-existing ideas.

Now I come to evidence that shows that cell-assemblies do exist and function in perception as the theory proposed. Defects in the theory also show up, but suggest new possibilities for cognitive learning. The result is to relate learning and perception more intimately. To simplify, perception in the early stages is a consequence of a primitive learning process, but thereafter learning becomes a function of perception—the learning, that is, that is most characteristic of the adult human being—and a function of cognitive structures that originate in perception.

THE STABILIZED-IMAGE EXPERIMENTS

My doubts about cell-assembly theory were abolished by a brilliant set of experiments by Roy Pritchard and Woodburn Heron (Pritchard, 1961; Pritchard, Heron & Hebb, 1960) that opened a new page in the study of perception. They put a decisive limitation on certain holistic ideas from Gestalt psychology but also gave new and stronger support for other Gestalt propositions.

The background of the research is as follows. There is always some tremor of the muscles that control the movement of the eyeball in its socket, and consequently some slight movement of the image, on the retina, of what is looked at, even though one tries to keep one's gaze fixed. R. W. Ditchburn and L. A. Riggs independently discovered about 1952 that this slight movement of the image on the retina is necessary to normal vision, for when they managed to stabilize the image of a line crossing the visual field the line promptly disappeared, reappearing intermittently. When I heard about this, I saw that it was an obviously important discovery concerning visual sensation, but it was not related, apparently, to my ideas about cell-assemblies. But then I heard several years later of an experiment done by Pritchard in Ditchburn's laboratory in England. A somewhat more complex object was looked at instead of a single line, and it did not disappear all at once; instead, different parts disappeared and reappeared, and what part disappeared was affected by what the observer attended to.

This was a different matter, with a direct bearing on the theory. The theory said that attention is a selective support for some sensory inputs and not others, thus determining what is perceived at any particular time. Disappearance of part of the object must mean that the assembly concerned, or group of assemblies, is fatigued or inhibited and has stopped firing. *When* this happens must be affected by the supporting activity of other assemblies. Theoretically, the support might prolong activity, or by increasing the activity within the assembly might hasten the onset of fatigue (my informant had reported that the part of the object attended to disappeared sooner; in our own subsequent research this effect was sometimes obtained, but more frequently attention had the effect of keeping the part-object visible longer). Here was a way of getting direction information about assembly activity and the interaction of assemblies.

When Pritchard joined our research group at McGill he and Heron made a further development of a technique that Pritchard had already used in England. The target—the object to be observed—was attached by a short stalk directly to a contact lens on the observer's eye (cf. Figure 18) with a tiny collimating lens to let the target be seen as if at a comfortable distance. The targets were mostly line diagrams; a drawing was photographed and the transparency was trimmed to a size that would fit into the optical system on the contact lens.

The main problem of adaption for the subject was to learn not to be surprised when an object or part of an object in clear view suddenly disappeared or when something equally suddenly reappeared all at once—not

FIG. 18.   Sketch of contact lens and optical apparatus mounted on the eyeball
of the reclining observer. The wire taped to the forehand of the subject connects
with a tiny lamp to illuminate the target. Based on a photograph in
Pritchard (1961).

gradually, but as a whole—since the result of surprise was a jerky movement
of the eyes that disturbed the position of the contact lens and so destabilized
the retinal image. I will not try to report all the dramatic results that Pritchard
and Heron obtained before I was invited by them to have a contact lens fitted
so I could observe them myself. A sample of those that gave direct evidence of
the activity of cell-assemblies is found in Figure 19. With outline drawings,
straight lines without intersection acted, in perception, as units, disappearing
or reappearing all at once. This is in full agreement with the proposition that
the perception of a single line is the activity of a cell-assembly, as a system that
is active as a whole or else inactive (Hebb, 1963). This essentially is the
evidence that demonstrates the existence of cell-assemblies.

In Figure 20 on the other hand appear results showing that the theory of
how assemblies work is not satisfactory as it has been presented. For example,
the completion in perception of an incomplete triangle is stronger support for
Gestalt ideas of this kind than any previously available, but the fact that the
completion is thinner, less vivid, than the rest of the line as perceived, conflicts
with the idea that the perception of a line is the activity of a cell-assembly,

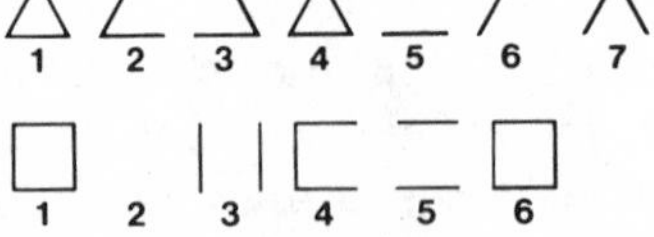

FIG. 19.   Two sample sequences of patterns perceived with stabilized images;
above, triangle as target; *below*, square. The sequence of course is variable
from one time to the next. The blank space in position 2, *below*, signifies
complete disappearance of the square, followed by partial regeneration.

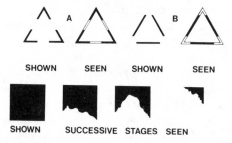

FIG. 20. Difficulties for the theory. *Above, A,* the target triangle with incomplete sides (left) is perceived complete but the completions are fainter than the rest of the triangle; *B,* similarly when it is the apices of the triangle that are missing. The completions agree with theory, but the faintness does not. *Below,* the square disappears gradually, unlike the outline square of Figure 19; this too is inconsistent with the theory. The postulate of subassemblies may remove the difficulties.

without qualification. If the activity is all-or-none the line as perceived cannot vary in faintness or vividness. The fact of completion supports the cell-assembly idea, since the idea was that the assembly activity meant perceiving a line of indefinite length running continuously across the field, but the loss of vividness does not, and now another difficulty appeared: How can an *incomplete* line be seen? The theory offered no possibility of seeing a gap in a line, nor the end of a line in central vision. Obviously we do perceive incomplete lines and their endings, so here the theory was grossly defective. Finally, among these pieces of contradictory evidence, it was found that a solid or filled-in diagram such as the square of Figure 20 disappeared gradually when seen with stabilized image, vanishing slowly like a piece of cheese being nibbled away by a mouse, and the theory in its original form had no way of dealing with that effect.

However, the theory is improvable. The defects are not fatal. (1) In the first place, the existence of a neural inhibition was not definitely known in 1949 and was not incorporated in the theory though it would have helped. Peter Milner (1957) showed how to incorporate it, making the first improvement. (2) A further improvement is to assume that an assembly comprises a number of subassemblies, temporarily cohering with other circuits in a single system; and finally, (3) add to the latter assumption a proposal concerning the mechanism of that temporary "coherence"—the proposal, however, being supported by other evidence of transient associations in cognitive learning. In this respect, the need of improving the theory with respect to perception leads to a way of dealing with a long-standing but disregarded problem of the learning and memory that result from momentary stimulations.

We will return later to the first point concerning inhibition, which may be as essential to intellectual activity as Sir Charles Sherrington showed it to be for reflex activity. On (2), it seems that the difficulties just discussed can be dealt with by assuming that the perception of a line in the visual field depends on the excitation, by the line, of an elongated narrow set of subassemblies in the striate cortex (the primary visual area), as well as excitation of peristriate circuits activated by that particular combination of subassemblies and helping in return to maintain their activity. It must be assumed, if this is to account for the facts, that the subassembly has a very small extent in terms of visual angle, bordering on the microscopic in relation to the extent of the visual field. Variations in vividness or intensity of the line as perceived result from differences in the proportion of subassemblies that are active within the cortical region that the line excites. The perception of finer or coarser lines becomes intelligible in the same way. And so with the perception of an imcomplete line, with associated implicit motor activation of the eye muscles or actual eye movement. And, last of the difficulties listed above, the gradual fading of solid figures such as the square of Figure 20 becomes intelligible, as the density of excitation—the proportion of subassemblies that are active in the stimulated area—decreases with inhibition or fatigue.

The third point is the mechanism by which subassemblies and the peristriate circuits cohere to form a single system: transient, but momentarily functional. The proposal in brief is that any discrete cortical or cortico-subcortical organized activities excited together—assemblies or subassemblies —tend to be reciprocally exciting, forming one larger pattern of activity because transmission of excitation at the synapses connecting them tends to keep the synapses "open" and active for some short period of time. On this basis, subassemblies that have often been active together, and have excited peristriate circuits connecting them, may constitute a unified cell-assembly whose activity is ended only by inhibition.

COGNITIVE ASSOCIATION AND INHIBITION

Now to consider that third point—the immediate but temporary cohering of subassemblies—and some related phenomena of cognitive association.

The commonest form of human learning is the immediate one-trial association of one perceptual event with another or with the ongoing cognitive background activity such as an awareness of where one is. The associations that psychology has emphasized so much—and to which, as a basis of higher behavior, such strong objection has been made—are ones that depend on repeated exposure, as in conditioning. The one-trial associations we are concerned with here are quite different in that respect and must depend on a different mechanism. A glimpse of a clouded sky or a word or two from a radio weather report is enough to let one know that there is no hope of sunbathing, and one does not have to rehearse a verbal response ("it's cloudy, it's cloudy, it's cloudy, . . . ") to establish the learning. In the news is a reference to a person or event of no interest at the time, but a few minutes later someone tells you something that makes it of interest and the reference is recalled. Learning took place. Or you see a car and later can report its color or the direction it was being driven. The information mostly is not retained long, but perception is constantly providing you with *knowledge*, transient or lasting. Obviously, it is not setting up specific response tendencies—you are not learning then to *do* something—but makes a modification of cortical function that means, in turn, modification of the way you will respond in any of an indefinite number of possible situations in the future. As I have said, this is the commonest form of adult human learning. It occurs constantly during waking hours, and it has been totally disregarded by learning theory.

Laboratory-style control of the phenomenon is possible with the repetition of digits, which is not as well understood as the lack of theoretical interest in it might let one think. Ask an experimental subject to repeat a set of digits such as 1-2-3-6-4-5 and he does so with ease; but how does he do it, in view of all his past practice with 1-2-3-4-5-6? That counting sequence must be highly overlearned, the synaptic modifications on which it depends must be strongly established, and yet the new sequence is organized instantaneously, though usually not permanently, of course. Apparently in the same way, you see a pencil lying on the shelf and associate the two perceptions, of pencil and of shelf, so that ten minutes later when you hear someone ask "Where's the pencil?", you are able to answer.

The repetition of digits in a unfamiliar order may be possible only because the cell-assemblies concerned became temporarily connected when they are excited in close temporal contiguity, and remembering the whereabouts of the pencil similarly because of a connection between assemblies constituting the percept of the pencil and those whose activity is the awareness of its locus, solely because they are simultaneously active. What explanation is there?

In 1949 it was considered that a neuron fired once would be harder to fire a second time, and consequently, that transmission at the synapse would increase in difficulty with repetition. The use of microelectrodes, directly recording activity of individual neurons in the central nervous system (a great body of research that began in the early 1950s), showed instead that a neuron fired once is more likely to fire again, and synaptic transmission temporarily facilitates further transmissions (Douglas & Goddard, 1975). This makes intelligible, physiologically, an immediate temporary coalescence of activity in two or more cell-assemblies or assembly groups. It is implied that there must be multiple synaptic connections available, ready to be activated, but this must be the result of a complex early experience. It is consistent with the fact that the transient associations are possible only with familiar materials (it is easy to repeat a few words or the names of digits in your own language, but not when foreign words are used).

This makes a fundamental change in the concept of the cell-assembly itself. There is a new problem to deal with if the assembly, once activated, tends to go on firing. Here inhibition enters the picture, with a contribution to make to the level of cognitive functioning.

The same microelectrode methods that showed continued firing by the neuron also showed the existence of inhibition as a direct suppression of activity in one neuron by the activity of another (Eccles, 1953). At least some of the closed loops of the cortex (Figure 11, p. 85) must have the function of suppressing activity in the system, not maintaining it. I have already referred to the possibility that the high efficiency of the human brain, in comparison with its weight, may be the result of the great frequency of Ramón y Cajal's short-axon (or local-circuit) neurons that appear to be inhibitory (p. 52). They may have the function of promptly shutting off a cell-assembly once it has acted to fire the next assembly of an internal sequence or, once it has made its contribution to a motor act, controlling the duration of firing in the separate sets of efferent fibers leading to motor centers. A maintained psychological state or process (an image or a concept) is more likely to be a function of a closed cycle or reverberation among a set of assemblies than of reverberation within the assembly itself.

Thought is a sequence of activities. When one of the events in the sequence has done its job of exciting the next it should cease promptly; otherwise it must be disruptive, like an actor who keeps on repeating his speech after it has provided the cue for the next actor's speech. If A is to fire B and B fire C, and A keeps on firing B after the time for B's function has passed, it must prevent a smooth flow in the sequence of events. At the least, it must make thought woolly and inefficient but at the worst—if this happens widely throughout the cerebrum—must grossly disorganize the thought process. A built-in inhibition to shut a cell-assembly off as soon as it has fired will prevent that possibility, and it becomes intelligible that the remarkable power of the human brain is accounted for by the "prodigious abundance" of short-axon neurons that so impressed Ramón y Cajal, if these neurons are inhibitory or if many of them are.

It is also possible, incidentally, that these small unmyelinated neurons are more vulnerable than others to anoxia, especially at birth, and that the syndrome of "minimal brain damage" or "dysfunction" (where behavioral disorder in the growing child makes birth injury seem likely but no specific loss can be demonstrated) is one result. It is suspected that eidetic imagery is a product of a slight degree of brain damage, and eidetic imagery is the vivid reinstatement of a percept, briefly, after the object perceived has been removed from sight (Hebb, 1968). I also find personally that with advancing age I am bothered more by the phenomenon of words "running through my head," in the familiar phrase, or the persistent return of my thought to a topic I would as soon forget till I can do something about it. This is a common phenomenon but it has become worse with age, and that may be the result of a selective loss of inhibitory neurons: possible evidence that they are more fragile.

COGNITIVE DEVELOPMENT

The newborn infant starts out with a well-developed reflex capability, which may give a false impression of conscious awareness. Fantz (1961) showed for example that when the baby's eyes are exposed to a diagram in an otherwise blank background, he will focus on the diagram rather than the blank area and with different diagrams will focus oftener and longer on one than on the other. This looks as though the baby is perceiving, and prefers some diagrams to others. But that does not follow. The eyes move reflexively in response to retinal stimulation and the behavior does not necessarily show anything except that a diagram is a more effective reflex excitant than a plain surface, and that some patterns are more exciting than others.

For some psychologists the emphasis on learning in cell-assembly theory is unacceptably empiricist, with too much talk of learning and too little recognition of the innate. But that emphasis is a strategy, not the expression of a conviction. With reasonable certainty, one can say that eventually we will know as much about the operation of genetic factors in the determination of behavior as we do about the operation of experience, but that day has not yet come. An essential source of information about the innate factor is finding out within what constraints learning operates, what is learned easily as well as what needs no learning, and what can be learned only with difficulty or not at all.

Cell-assembly theory supposes that cognitive development begins at zero, at birth or conceivably somewhat before birth though to no great extent. But it does not give experience a blank slate to write on (or to develop the metaphor, if blank, the slate has grooves and indentations that make the appearance of some letters inevitable, other letters impossible). In the case of visual perception, what assemblies develop and become the basis of perception is fully dependent on an innate property of the organism, the reflex responsiveness of the eye muscles, as well as on the innately determined structure of the striate and peristriate cortex which—according to the theory—is what makes the formation of cell-assemblies inevitable, given exposure to a normal visual environment. To take this further, learning is involved in the functional relation between parallel lines that makes it possible for larger and smaller similar triangles, or similar triangles in different parts of the visual field, to be perceived as similar—and to evoke the same naming response, for example—since the triangles are composed of three sets of parallel lines. But this is not empiricism any more than nativism. The learning is inevitable in view of the responsiveness of the eye to peripheral stimulation, and the fact that the resulting eye sweep causes parallel rows of excitation across the retina wherever there are points of light in the visual field. According to the theory, it is this relation between the organism and its environment that produces a functional identity of horizontal lines anywhere in the field, or an identity of vertical lines. Certain kinds of visual learning are determined in advance, by the way the organism is constructed, and recognizing this puts no more emphasis on experience than on innate properties.

Another example of great interest has to do with the development of language. Condon and Sander (1974) have shown that the newborn baby is selectively responsive to the rhythms of human speech, innately prepared for and impelled toward a form of learning that, we know, is inevitable in normal conditions: that is, learning to talk. Exposed to the sound of speech, there is a correspondence in "microanalysis" (taking behavioral segments of about 1/10 sec duration) of fine movements by the baby with spoken language, whether English or Chinese. No such correspondence was found with the sound of tapping or isolated vowel sounds. The baby is built to react to verbal stimulation, *predisposed* for learning language.

Such predispositions are bound to be hard to demonstrate directly. Holloway's (1974) paleological evidence suggests an early divergence of the evolutionary path of brain structure toward the distinctive human pattern, and the known facts of that pattern—lateralization and localization of verbal function, usually in the left hemisphere—clearly mean the existence of an extensive innate factor in language, but it would certainly not be possible to show this experimentally and there is little likelihood of being able to observe it naturalistically, by direct observation. It is hard to see how remarkable things are that we all share. There is nothing extraordinary about language—any baby can learn it, where's the problem?—and it took a Chomsky to make us realize how great in fact the problem is. It might have been seen at once by a visitor from outer space, with a different cognitive structure; or analysis of the language-learning of human infants by human adults might have been made easier if the analyst had some babies from outer space for comparison, with aptitudes as complex but not the same as those that make language-learning easy for the human baby. If babies are all so to speak equipped with slates that have special grooves and slots for auditory experience—innate modes of receiving certain classes of sounds and fixing and relating them to other experience—then anything that experience writes on those slates will have certain features in common. But the babies' elders started out with the same slots and they must be hard to discover, for the learning they control is so "natural" that its peculiarities will be evident only by the light of theory, slowly developing.

Let us return to the cell-assembly. The same innate cortical structure and function that permits postulation of the formation, by a learning process, of the elementary assemblies that have been discussed so far make it possible also to postulate the existence of higher-order assemblies whose activity is the basis of abstraction and generalization in thought. What I have talked about so far is the first-order assembly whose activity is the awareness of such perceptual elements as a contour in the visual field, a pressure on the skin at some point, a simple taste, a noise of particular pitch, and so on. When one of these events happens repeatedly, those neurons that are often excited by it will organize to form an assembly. (In vision, there is reason, as we have seen, to think that the assembly comprises subassemblies, and the same thing may occur elsewhere. For example, it could account for differences of intensity in the perception of a note of given pitch or of pressure at a particular point on the skin.) When the theory was in the course of construction, about 1945, I realized that the facts on which the cell-assembly was based also implied the possibility of what I then called a superordinate assembly. When a group of assemblies are repeatedly activated, simultaneously or in sequence, those cortical cells that are regularly active following that primary activity may themselves become organized as a superordinate (second-order) assembly. The activity of this assembly then is representative of that combination of events that individually organized the first-order assemblies. After a baby has developed assembly activities for lines of different slope in the visual field and then is repeatedly exposed to some triangular object—to take the simplest possible example—the combinations of activity of the three assemblies may lead to the formation of a higher-order assembly whose activity is the perception of the triangular object rather than its three sides as such. This might be a second-order assembly if the object is seen always in the same orientation, or a third-order assembly formed in the same way by the repeated excitation of second-order assemblies, fired by seeing the object in different orientations.

This elaboration of the theoretical scheme seems highly speculative, but it has physiological support. There is no point in trying to elaborate too much detail, however, because the possibilities are too varied. For example, it seems that superordinate perceptions are likely to develop from the stimulations of such a familiar object as a toy animal or mother's face or hand before any such artificial idea as that of a triangular shape develops, although for purposes of exposition it was possible to be clearer with that example. My concern here is to show at least in principle the possibility that higher-order assemblies are the basis of abstract ideas. And in that attempt a most effective support comes from the work of Hubel and Wiesel (1962), who have demonstrated physiologically a hierarchy of neurons in the visual system. Simple cells are ones that are excited directly by a line or contour of a specific slope in a specific part of the visual field; complex cells are excited by simple cells; and hypercomplex cells are excited by complex cells. A complex cell is fired by any of a number of simple cells that vary somewhat in locus. Thus its activity is generalization on a small scale, since it makes the same response to different sensory stimuli; and it is also abstraction, since there is transmission of only one kind of information about the sensory stimulation (i.e., slope of line is included, locus is omitted). The parallel of simple, complex, and hypercomplex (and at least one of still higher order) with first, second, third, and probably fourth-order cell-assemblies is obvious. Hubel and Wiesel's research makes the existence of higher-order cell-assemblies a considerably less speculative idea.

From all we know, this is the kind of complexity that is demanded of the brain of the growing child. Scott (1977) regards as conservative an estimate that one billion (10^9) cell-assemblies are formed in a normal human brain in the course of ordinary experience. That may be a conservative estimate, but it represents the formation of assemblies at the rate of one per second for 30 years, sleeping time included, or for 45 years counting only 16 hours per day. This it appears is what makes possible the normal development of intelligence and the human learning capacity, including the capacity for abstracting and generalizing, and being able to see the wood instead of the trees—seeing the larger pattern as well as the detail—that is fundamental to human thought.

PERCEPTION IN THE DEVELOPMENT
OF LANGUAGE

This is not the place, and I am not the author, to attempt any systematic treatment of language. Nevertheless, the theory of cell-assemblies has clear implications concerning language-learning and I must point to some of these and, if I can, go far enough into the topic to interest the psycholinguist in its possibilities.

Hebb, Lambert, and Tucker (1971) dealt with the question with the aim of avoiding the extremes of nativism on the one hand and empiricism on the other. What follows is based on that discussion, which built largely on perception and the memory image that results from perception. Three main points: Elaborate perceptual learning must precede both comprehension and use of words; a general concept of a name (nounness) is intelligible on the basis of a relation between heard names and seen objects, and similarly with action words (verbness); and with imagery a basis of active-passive transformations becomes understandable.

First, in learning to name an object, the theory does not allow us even to consider the beginning of language as a direct association between the sight of an object and the motor response. The child must first learn separately to *perceive* both word and object, with the development of auditory and visual cell-assemblies of lower and higher order. Now a connection becomes possible between the auditory perceptual complex excited when the mother says "doggie," for example, and the complex excited by the sight of a dog. This is not S-R but S-S learning—not stimulus-response but a sensory-sensory or more accurately a perceptual-perceptual association.

But we must take account of the response capacity also. To provide for the child's ability to say "doggie" himself we must assume that the basis for motor learning is being laid at the same time. As the child hears his own vocalizations, more or less random at first, connections are built up between the resultant auditory stimulations and the concurrent vocalizations: a threadbare idea but still possible. As the speech of adults becomes familiar and the child begins to perceive the constituent phonemes and phoneme combinations, that auditory stimulation must have a shaping effect on the child's own vocalizations and make them approximate closer and closer to the adult patterns. The result is a tendency to repeat a spoken word and, because of the S-S association referred to above, to name a seen object—to the extent that object and name are already familiar.

That circular-reflex type of explanation looks like the revival of an idea long dead and buried. All that saves it from banality is the accompanying notion that the process is effective only in combination with the proposed extensive perceptual learning. This is the problem of imitation; instead of making imitation the key to language-learning, the proposal shows that imitation itself must be accounted for first, a product of a prolonged period of mostly latent learning whose first effect is comprehension, well before the appearance of talking.

Second, consider the concept of a name and what Slobin (1966) has called "nounness". Fundamental to this is the generalized idea of a thing, an object, a space-occupying and sense-stimulating *something,* as the activity of a higher-order cell-assembly made up of neurons that are usually or always active in the relatively small number of different situations of infancy when a visible, tangible object attracts attention. Those neurons must be a small proportion of the total number excited on any one of such occasions but may still be a large number in absolute terms. The theoretical possibility of such an assembly is clear and the psychological support for its existence is also clear. The highly abstract idea of something, a thing or event with little specification other than its existence and perhaps its function or effect, is a thoroughly familiar one and an important component of thought in many situations. It appears early ("What are those *things,* Mommy?") and is common at maturity; consider such terms as thingummybob, *je ne sais quoi,* and gadget or gismo, this last definable as an ingenious something with which to do something or get some effect.

Parallel with that idea of a thing is the idea of a name. Many neurons are excited every time the mother's vocalization coincides with the appearance of an attention-getting object or with some action by the mother that draws attention to a particular object. The small proportion that are common to these excitations, organized in an assembly and concurrent with the assembly complex that is the idea of a thing, form the idea of a name. Now the child perceives the mother's vocalization both as a particular word related to a particular object, and as a name. In the same way the general idea of something happening—organized activity of neurons common to perceptions of things moving or changing—is paralleled by generalization from hearing the accompanying words, such as *run, cry, fall, drink.* The child develops meaning for the individual words but also develops the higher-order concept of a reference to (observable) activity. This is the first stage of the development of nounness and verbness.

In the second stage there is a further generalization. Familiar with "Bobby is crying," "Bobby is running," and so on, the child hears a new word not associated with observable action but in a familiar verbal setting: "Bobby is sleeping," and *sleep* is heard as an action word even though no action is visible. Besides exciting the idea or image of the immobile Bobby, as seen, it excites the higher-order cell-assembly that has already been built up by *run, cry* and so on—the abstract idea of verbness, now generalized. Note however: The theory says that what assembly group is excited by a particular sensory stimulation is a function also of the context. In another verbal context ("Sleep is good for Bobby," for example) the same word will acquire nounness, and context will continue to be decisive in determining which property the word sleep has in future situations—which higher-order assembly it will excite.

Nounness and verbness at first sound like esoteric and fanciful ideas, remote from the world of science and the study of behavior, but in fact a physiological meaning can be assigned to them—a meaning that is at least intelligible and one that is possibly true.

And third, of these illustrative possibilities, is a theoretical basis for the relation of active to passive voice, which has been a problem. This is found in the fluidity of perception and memory image. As one surveys a scene of activity the focus of one's attention varies from moment to moment, and verbal report may vary accordingly. When agent A impinges on target T at a moment when attention is on T the perceptual sequence is *percept of T—impact from A.* Verbal report may then tend to take the same pattern, "T was hit by A"; but if instead attention had been on A, with perceptual sequence *percept of A—movement by A—impact on T,* report might tend instead to be "A hit T." This is not a rigid theoretical inference—other factors may operate—but it does show how the different speech forms, active and passive, are determined by different perceptions—of the same event. Similarly with the memory image: When Johnny is called on to report playground violence, he may recall the scene beginning with the aggressor so the report takes the form "Billy hit Kathy," but if Kathy is the center of interest for him at the time of report, it would take the form "Kathy was hit by Billy."

These proposals, which attempt to show the relevance for psycholinguistics of cell-assembly theory with its emphasis on perception and representative process (image and idea, or assemblies of lower and higher order), must not be taken to mean simplification of the problems. If the theory makes the idea of nounness intelligible physiologically or shows how another approach may be made to the difficult problem of active-passive transformations, what it does is substitute one complexity for another, and the new one is manifestly no less complex than the old. The general conception relates the controlling processes of verbal and nonverbal behavior more intimately, and denies that psycholinguistics can pursue its problems successfully without regard for the theory of perception and of thought generally, but that complicates rather than simplifies the problem.

8 The Structure of Thought

The classical theory of thought as an association of ideas seems to have been shaped by certain assumptions that now look primitive. They were not usually made explicit and perhaps were regarded as obvious facts, not theoretical postulates that needed to be put into words and justified.

Thus: Images are a fact of common experience, an image is simply a percept occurring in the absence of the thing that seems to be perceived, and images like percepts occur one by one; so, using the term *idea* to comprise both percept and image, thought appears to be a linear series of ideas—that is, ideas one after another in single file. But thinking includes abstractions and generalizations also, and these are not images (no image embodies the general idea of *bigness,* and no one image can represent an *animal* in view of the fact that animals include frogs, snakes, elephants, and beetles). Such ideas must be words only. Putting this in behavioristic terms, "big" is a verbal response separately conditioned to the sight of big people, big houses, big books; "animal" has its general significance only as a separately made response to a number of different animate objects. If the verbal response is not overt it must be an auditory image. Thought then becomes a series of images in which verbal images have a special function (which leads directly to the common idea, even today, that thought is essentially verbal).

To this scheme, as we know, there was strong opposition. It held the field against criticism, however, for it had one great strength. The criticisms were devastating, but there was no theoretical alternative. There were indeed other views; in 1890 James gave a better account of thought, but only as a description or a statement of what it was that had to be explained; twenty years later Külpe established the fact of imageless thought but again without explanation (what else could thought be, if not images?). Like Gestalt psychology somewhat later, James and Külpe were playing the invaluable critic's role of keeping the theorist in touch with reality, but not at all attempting to take his place. Failing an alternative, the theory of the association of ideas held the field, until the Behaviorist revolution substituted an association of stimulus with response for the association of one mental event with another. In that revolution, images and ideation were lost—as we have seen, because Watson listened to the physiologists, and the physiologists had a conception of the brain that allowed no autonomy of function. Today physiology has reversed its field, not only showing that autonomous activity exists but also opening the door to a more adequate account of the interaction and association of representative processes.

The defects of the earlier theory were not due to the postulate of association—the proposition that ideas excited together tend subsequently to excite one another—for no theory can account of human learning without that proposition in one form or another. The defects mainly originated in (1) the (tacit) notion that thought is a linear series of ideas, and (2) a very limited notion of the nature of an idea. The first of these sources of trouble leads to what has been known as the problem of the direction of thought; the second we return to a little later, along with the problem of creativity. And finally, we can ask how all this relates to the recent and remarkable discoveries of Hilgard in the field of hypnosis.

THE DIRECTION OF THOUGHT

The classical problem of the direction of thought is to understand how thought can stick to one topic long enough to reach a conclusion. A simple linear series of accidental associations would certainly deviate promptly. For example, you think of an experiment you would like to do, *experiment* is associated with *lab,* which is associated with laboratory *table,* which is associated with *leg,* which is associated with *nylons,* which is associated with *girls*—and, lo and behold, the experiment is lost forever. The example is a caricature but it makes the point, that a chain of ideas in which each link is determined by whatever association of the previous link happens at that moment to be strongest can contain no guiding principle.

But there is no reason to assume that thought is such a linear series, whatever introspection may seem to testify. In fact, there is behavioral evidence to show that at least two streams of thought, in William James' figure of speech, may flow at the same time; one can drive a car and talk sensibly at the same time, and anyone who has spent much time reading aloud with light material such as stories for children knows that at times other thoughts obtrude without interrupting the reading. Neither driving a car nor reading *Little Red Ridinghood* is intellectually demanding, but each does require a constant perceptual and cognitive activity. It is only ancient dogma that thought must be unitary. There must be great numbers of cell-assemblies simultaneously active in thought, whether in one stream or two. The probability of radical fluctuation from moment to moment, consequently, is slight, with the net effect of many unitary associations; and the continued directedness, to the extent that there is direction—often enough there is not—may also be owing to the persistent activity of a smaller group of strongly established higher-order assemblies.

For it is easy to overdo the notion of a directedness in thought, self-maintained and not dependent on the persistence of a biological need such as thirst, or on the continued reminder of something in the environment such as the clock you were going to repair or the tools you have assembled to repair it with. James' analogy of the stream of thought is misleading in its implication of a steadily progressive flow of ideas from start to finish, from problem to solution. That sort of progression happens only with familiar problems and well-known modes of attack. Otherwise, a better comparison would be with the behavior of a hound on a faint trace, casting about when the trace is lost and repeatedly coming back even to the starting point in order to pick it up again. Directedness in that sense is readily accounted for as the result of persisting activity in some cell-assemblies and the ready re-activation of others.

Related to the same question is the problem of "noise" in cerebral function, and the difficulty, familiar to every student, of sticking to one line of thought: the difficulty, that is, of concentrating. Concentration clearly is a state in which one set of cortical activities continues, not disrupted by other irrelevant activities that, figuratively, are noise, and this is a problem in a brain such as the human being's.

It may be overlooked that having a big brain is not always a help in the performance of any one task. The value of a big brain is that many different things can be learned and retained, and higher-order cell-assemblies can be developed that are not possible in a smaller brain; but there must be many more neurons than are needed for any one learning assignment, and the evidence is clear that though much neural tissue may be necessary to develop a higher-order concept, the concept may be retained and function with much less tissue—that is, fewer neurons—following cortical damage (Hebb, 1949, p.291). This means that there is a large number of neurons at any time whose activity is not necessary for the current thought process. But the neuron is alive and fires spontaneously when not excited from without, given its proper job of conducting excitation from one point to another. Activity by those excess neurons firing at random would have to be disruptive of the concurrent organized activity, since they must outnumber the organized ones. How then can organized thought continue?

Inhibition may be the answer, but this is unlikely. It is hardly plausible that a smaller organized group of neurons can selectively inhibit a larger number, unorganized, especially since each of these two populations changes from moment to moment as thought proceeds, necessary neurons becoming unnecessary and unnecessary ones necessary. The only apparent answer is to suppose that the organized activity tends to recruit cell-assemblies widely and make their activity part of itself. The result may be a more extensive activity than the minimum requirement, but on the other hand a large safety factor is provided to ensure continuity in the ongoing thought process. The controlling idea of the task—the classical conception of the *Aufgabe* as a directing influence—becomes more complex and may make the task a more interesting one in consequence. An interesting task by definition is one that takes control of thought and maintains it, and the interest from the thinker's point of view may lie in seeing new angles of the problem, detecting internal relations or parallels with other problems, finding new patterns in the data, and so forth.

That recruitment, physiologically, and seeing new properties of the task, psychologically, can be possible only with a past history of complex associative connections between the various mental activities as well as complex perceptual learning so that a sensory input may excite higher-order as well as a varied lower-order assembly activity. The growth, intellectually, that makes sustained attention to a task possible is then a matter of first developing such assemblies, and second, establishing associative connections between them as threads of a tapestry are interwoven in making a larger pattern. The richness of interconnection must be a function of the early environment—which casts further light on the role of the environment in the development of normal intelligence. We can better understand why schooling is only an adjunct to the home and to the child's experience outside of school; for however good the school it can hardly provide that variety of past experience that is required for effective thought, if these proposals are sound.

CONTENT AND FORMATION OF IDEAS

The theory thus far developed says that representative processes, the content of thought, exist at several levels of abstraction, that these are both verbal and nonverbal, and that an idea or a memory image is not simple and static but a dynamic complex (after-images are not included since they depend on a continued sensory input). "Representative process" here includes both image and idea. The *image* is regarded as lower-order cell-assembly activity (first or second order) since it has a perceptual quality—one seems to see or hear or otherwise sense a particular object or event. The *idea* is regarded as the activity of higher-order assemblies, at a more abstract level. The distinction is rough and I have not adhered to it rigidly in some of my discussion, but it is useful in some situations.

Treating abstraction as the activity of higher-order assemblies theoretically permits the conclusion that elaborate thought may exist without verbal components, but this of course does not mean that verbal thought does not exist or that it is minimal. Since it is clear that there is thought in the higher mammals that lack language, we must suppose that nonverbal thought appeared in human evolution before any verbal thought and so is more fundamental. Also, nonverbal processes are still important, as in those situations where communication is difficult. If complex thought must be verbal, in content and organization, how can one have difficulty finding the words and the sequence of words to communicate it to another mind; how can a short-story writer know that a story is building up within but not be able yet to put any of it on paper; or how could A.E. Housman have a "vague notion" of part of a poem yet to be put into words? (Ghiselin, 1955, p. 91). So nonverbal thought may exist at a high level, even with reference to an ultimately verbal performance. But anyone who writes knows that having to put one's ideas in words can sharpen thought, and even on occasion lead to the discovery of error, and it seems obvious that the talking to oneself that goes on in any difficult task is not mere accompaniment but overflow from an active part of the thought. Language is the outstanding distinctive mark of human behavior and this, it seems, may be true of human thought also.

As for "dynamic complexity," the theory says that what one would ordinarily speak of as an idea is the activity of a changing set of cell-assemblies, a constant flux on any one occasion and variable in its make-up on different occasions, in different contexts. Much of the sterility of the 19th-century theory of the association of ideas came from thinking of thought as made up of unchanging images, verbal and nonverbal, each of which was the reinstatement of a particular perceptual event—the conception that William James made fun of, comparing the temporary reappearance to that of the Jack of Spades, unchanged on each occasion. His denial that the same idea ever recurs may be extreme, but considering what has been said above in connection with the *Aufgabe,* it may not be. The present theory certainly points in the same direction.

Old difficulties for association theory become less difficult when one thinks of even simple ideas as complex and made up of a number of part-ideas. The strong association of opposites such as *black-white* or *up-down* and the association by similarity or contrast are easy to understand if in each case the two ideas share common elements as well as containing others that serve to keep them distinct. The evidently important role of analogy in scientific as well as everyday thought also becomes more understandable. It is betrayed by the pervasive figures of speech in both cases. In science they are everywhere: sound *waves,* a *fall* in blood sugar *level,* the *cell* in botany, the *thrust* of enormous masses of rock in geology, a *front* in meterology, and so forth. The idea of a water wave is a complex including sub-ideas of the regular repetition and alternation of opposite states (up and down or high and low), each of these itself a complex. Whoever first thought of sound as a rhythmic alternation of opposites (compression and rarefaction) had, in the familiar idea of a water wave, a cognitive framework into which to fit the new idea, as the idea of a water wave with certain differences ("schema with correction"). The use of the term *wave* in these two very different contexts therefore is not "mere analogy," superficial and misleading, but represents a cognitive reality. As for the comparable role of analogy in everyday speech, I need give few examples: *running* water, the house that *caught* fire, a *balanced* budget, feeling *low,* the time is *ripe,* the *depth* of winter followed by *spring* (i.e., an upward leap)—and I note even the fundamentally poetic language "in the *spring of the year*" and "in the *fall of the year*" to be heard occasionally from countrymen and farmers who would certainly disavow any poetic intention. In each case we may see a partial identity of thought, a shared abstraction.

The development of new concepts from this point of view is a process of modification and development of old ones, as far as adult thought is concerned, and the extent to which this is possible depends on what elaboration of the basic primitive components has gone on in childhood. We know there is some kind of cognitive growth (note that figure of speech, and the underlying analogy!) that tapers off (again!) somewhere about the age of 15—the "mental age" or MA of intelligence-test measurement—and what it consists of or how it differs from the subsequent cognitive development at maturity has been a puzzle. From our present point of view it may now be suggested that the first 10 or 15 years of life, the years in which the MA increases, are the period in which really new conceptual structures are formed, new cell-assemblies arising directly from sensory stimulation as well as new higher-order assemblies. The period is one in which both the structural pieces *and* the blueprints of subsequent thought develop. And this process may come to an end as perception is increasingly channelled and controlled by prior perceptual structures, the new wine now going into old bottles; in adult thought thereafter a new concept is always a reorganization of pre-existent ones, and the extent to which new ideas are possible is limited by the extent and variety of the early-formed and more primitive ones.

All this assumes a complexity and internal activity of even simple and familiar ideas. As an approach to the dynamics of an idea, look first at the dynamics of perception, from which—to paraphrase Locke—all concepts must originate even if—to interpret Leibnitz's rejoinder—the course of development is shaped by inborn rules.

Perception is an active process, not mere passive reception of information. There was a long period in which a percept, the end product of perceiving, was tacitly regarded as a static entity (static, because isomorphic with the external stimulating object). That notion was possible only because of preoccupation with familiar visual patterns which can be perceived at a glance, especially in the tachistoscope. The latter instrument gives a momentary exposure only, too brief for any eye movement. In real life perception is very different; even in looking at a familiar object one makes two or three fixations, or more, and with a strange object that investigative process may go on for seconds, even minutes, before one feels that one has really perceived it as a distinctive thing. Perception in that case is a series of inputs separated and controlled by motor eye movements. One might suppose that the eye movement is only a mechanical accompaniment, but there is evidence to argue strongly that the structure of a percept depends essentially on the motor links. Even when an object is recognized at a glance, the percept is still sequential, with motor links, except in those cases where the first part-perception immediately gives rise to some different mental activity—in which case the perceptual process ends before reaching completion.

The evidence involves imagery. It will be found that something as simple as a circle cannot be clearly imaged without eye movement, implicit or overt (imagined or actually made, the latter being much more likely). However, the movement need not follow a circular path. It will be found also that an object such as a car or a house, or even one as uncomplicated as a door or as small as a table-fork or a human hand, is not clearly imageable as a whole complete in detail but only as series of part-images. That the whole is there as a whole, static and complete in detail like a picture before the mind's eye, is illusion. Each part-image is separated from the next by an eye movement (as above, real or imagined) which has the effect of seeming to shift the gaze from one part of the object to another. What follows what, in this sequence, is determined by the intervening motor element—which therefore has an essential integrating function.

In all this the memory image behaves like the perception from which it originated, but two points should be noted. There is reason to think that the memory image includes little or none of the first-order cell-assembly activity that is the basis of—initiates—perception, although hallucination and eidetic image do (Hebb, 1968). The second point is that there are perceptual changes that need not be initiated by motor activity. This is most clearly shown with the ambiguous figure (Fig. 9). What one sees can change without eye movement, or before the movement begins, and we saw (p. 82) that related changes of perceptual content constantly occur in ordinary circumstances— as for example when you fix your gaze on some point in the room and are aware now of the color of the surface, now of the surface as part of the floor, now of its distance from the wall, now of a nearby shadow or discoloration— all without need to move your eyes. If the dynamics of perception do not always involve motor movement, then presumably the dynamics of ideation do not; and we may suppose that they are least operative with abstract ideas and higher-order cell-assemblies, most operative with the first-order assemblies of the eidetic image and hallucination.

From the point of view we have now arrived at, creativity is not a rare attribute but a normal feature of cognitive activity. As we will see there are several aspects to take acount of, but we can begin by schematizing the occurrence of a new idea as in Figure 21. A new idea in everyday situations— what color of paint would improve the looks of the dining room, how to avoid rusting of garden tools, a new use for a pocket calculator, a witticism that depends on a pun—is truly creative, but the best-documented cases come from the reports of scientists and mathematicians, so let us consider that Figure 21 represents the occurrence more or less at random of possible parts of a solution to a technical problem—that is, *A, C, E, F,* and so on represent ideas that occur and recur in the thinking of the problem-solver. These are the product of the "preparation period" that is emphasized by every writer dealing with this question of scientific problem-solving. Some are data, some are recollections of former attempted solutions, and some are quite unrelated to the problem in hand; but the thinker of course does not know for sure which are relevant and which irrelevant. These all are cell-assembly groups which fire and subside, fire and subside, fire and subside, till the crucial combination occurs. In the diagram, this is represented by *K-L-M* firing in that order, but without the firing of certain other assemblies. Activity of *K-L-*

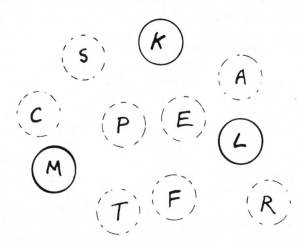

FIG. 21.   Illustrating a proposal concerning the creative idea. *A, C, E* and so on represent randomly firing cell-assembly groups which constitute the occurrence of ideas about the problem (they are of course not spatially separated as in the figure). The solution is represented by *K-L-M,* firing in that order. From D. O. Hebb, What psychology is about. *American Psychologist,* 1974, *29,* p. 77. Copyright 1974 by the American Psychological Association. Reprinted by permission.

M is the new scientific idea that sets off a new sequence of ideas or constitutes a different way of seeing the problem situation.

Simplistic this scheme may be, but it clarifies certain features of techinical discovery at once, as follows:

1. It explains why there is a chance element in discovery even for the prepared mind. The history of scientific discovery makes clear how great the chance element often is.

2. It makes understandable the *Eureka!* effect, as K-L-M "cohere" (p. 102) to form a functional system and so strongly excite the arousal system of the brain stem, because

3. The new system suddenly reorients the whole pattern of cortical activity, putting an end to the combinations and sequences of assembly activity that constitute the problem-solving phase in favor combinations and sequences that represent new possibilities opened up by the new idea. But

4. It is possible that K-L-M may occur in the right order and still not have such effects (K-L-M may not cohere to form the new system, perhaps because of inhibition from R or S firing at the same time, or perhaps because the necessary latent associative connections do not exist); they do not therefore cause the excitement of arousal nor reorient the course of cortical activity. The right idea has occurred but has not jelled and is lost. Thus

5. We can see why it is the wrong question to ask, "How does the thinker recognize a good idea when it occurs?" whereas the right question is, "What is the special property of a particular combination of part-ideas that makes it take control of all cortical activity from then on?" For

6. Not infrequently, a *wrong* answer may temporarily have that effect, and only be found to be wrong in the later testing. The thinker does not somehow inspect a new idea and see that it it good; instead, he finds himself (a) with a new sight of the problem situation and (b) excited. Only then does the realization follow that he has a solution, or at least a bright idea that he hopes will turn out to be the solution.

7. And from this point of view one can comprehend the sound but puzzling advice to the problem-solver, when he is stuck and can make no progress, to "think aside," or to get as far away as he can from the problem by engaging in other activity before coming back to it. For his thought is running in the wrong channels; the earlier bouts of thinking are likely to have strengthened interfering associations—for example, in Figure 21 a connection of K with R that blocks the sequence K-L-M—and a day or two or a month or two later the connection may have weakened enough to allow K to be active without R—that is, allow thought to proceed without that faulty presupposition. But of course the connection may not weaken, for some presuppositions are firmly grounded in earlier experience; or if it does, the chance factor in the occurrence of the effective combination K-L-M is still present. The scientific

record is clear that possessing a wrong idea can prevent one from seeing a solution that later seems obvious. Galileo knew about the weight of air but failed to solve the problem of the suction pump (why it can raise water only for 32 feet or so) presumably because of the well-established but false idea that Nature abhors a vacuum, and at one stage in his work Kepler had put together the solution for his problem of the orbit of Mars but could not see it because of taking certain other things for granted.

Thus the diagram of Figure 21 has some value as a first approximation to an account of creativity. The value depends on assuming that thought to some extent incorporates the dynamic aspects of perception. This line of inquiry can be followed further.

RELATING GESTALT PERCEPTUAL PHENOMENA TO SCIENTIFIC THOUGHT

Traditionally, it is induction that has received the most attention in philosophic discussion of the logical foundations of scientific thought. Here I hope to show that deduction is nearer the heart of the question and much more interesting. This will depend on a parallel between it and the perceptual phenomena of groups as entities, figure-ground relations, and pattern perception, first studied by Max Wertheimer and those who worked with him or followed him as Gestalt psychologists.

As a mode of discovery, induction is primitive. Its parallel is with association, as in the conditioned reflex, which requires little or no cognitive capacity and simply depends on repetition, which is quite within the capacity of mindless lower animals. The analogue of deduction is to be found in the restructuring of the perception of a complex field, which when it occurs is typically sudden and complete like a flash of insight. Such restructuring is known with certainty only in man, although it is reasonable to suppose that it is what lay behind the insightful changes of behavior in Köhler's chimpanzees (Köhler was not willing to commit himself on this point, presumably because it made difficulty for his conception of an isomorphism between percept and perceived situation). Peirce's third logical mode of abduction or retroduction—inference based on a hypothetical proposition—then finds its analogue in perceptual completions and the Gestalt conception of the good figure.

The first interesting consequence results from following up an apparent riddle posed in Hanson's *Patterns of Discovery* (1958). Hanson observes that two people looking at the same thing may see different things: Tycho Brahe for example and Johannes Kepler watching the sunrise, Tycho believing that the earth is still and the sun revolves about it, Kepler believing instead that the earth revolves about a fixed sun, and so they see different things.[12] A riddle, a paradox. But the word *see* is here used in a figurative sense. Any problem of interpretation disappears when we distinguish between sensation and perception: Tycho and Kepler see the same thing when the words have their primary meaning, but perceive differently (cf. Fig. 14). At least, they do so part of the time; at other times their perceptions, of the ball of fire and the patches and streaks of color in the clouds, are the same.

This is not mere hairsplitting. It brings us to a more far-reaching implication, which again is clearest with respect to the ambiguous figure which Hanson also deals with (though he mistakenly attributes it to Köhler instead of Rubin). Figure 9 is characteristically seen in *three* ways, not two. The observer perceives a vase alternating with profiles—and also a static configuration of lines on paper. It is static in the sense that it is perceived and thought of as the unchanging source of both the other perceptions, as something that remains the same while being perceived in different ways. In ordinary life the number of alternative potential ways of perceiving is greater—with a complex scene such as a city street or a garden or a living room, indefinitely large—but in principle the situation is the same: The scene is perceived as the unchanging background source of varying percepts, as attention changes from moment to moment.

Now apply this to the demonstration of certain arithmetical equalities which, treated verbally, are complex. Russell (1961, p. 786) for example, having remarked that the proposition $2 + 2 = 4$ cannot be proved by induction (by looking at many pairs of twos and finding that they are always counted as four), goes on to say: "But it is also not *a priori* knowledge about the world. It is in fact merely verbal knowledge," and adds that the proof is long. So it must be, in a merely verbal world of thought. But we have seen some reason to deny that all thought is verbal, and here is a further argument to the same effect, for the knowledge that two and two is four has a primitive perceptual basis.

As a preliminary to my argument, look now at Figure 22, and observe that it too can be perceived in more than one way. The various blobs may be seen (1) as a single group; (2) as three groups, a row of four at the top, curving upward to the right, a more or less horizontal row in the middle, and an

---

[12]Thus also, T. S. Kuhn (1962): "I am, for example, acutely aware of the difficulties created by saying that when Aristotle and Galileo looked at swinging stones, the one saw constrained fall, the second a pendulum" (p.220). But the difficulties are verbal. The sensations were in principle the same, the perceptions differed. As the ambiguous figure shows, the same sensations may give rise to different perceptions. Perception is a cortical process, a first stage of thought, and consequently interpretive; both Aristotle and Galileo saw the same thing—swinging stones—but in effect thought about it differently, which should surprise no one.

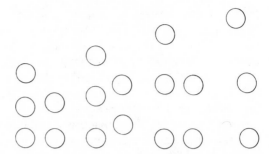

FIG. 22. To show Gestalt phenomena of grouping.

irregular bottom row slanting downward; (3) as three groups of five, counting
from left to right, followed by a widely spaced group at the end; and so on,
with a number of other possibilities. This is obvious enough, put into words,
but it is an aspect of perceptual dynamics that is so obvious that it may be
forgotten. With that preliminary, look at the top row of Figure 23. Here too
there are grouping phenomena, though less varied. As the bottom three rows
show, the top row may be perceived as a single on the left followed by a group
of three, or as two groups of two, or finally as a group of three followed by a
single on the right. (In other words, more verbally, *A B C D* may be seen as *A
BCD,* as *AB CD,* or as *ABC D.*) Intermittently, as the top row is being seen in
these different ways, it is also seen as an unchanging configuration of a set of
marks on paper. It is then perceptually evident that *the percept of four has the
same referent as the percept of two and two.* That is, one may perceive directly
that 2 and 2 are identical with 4 and, in view of the other two grouping shown
in the diagram, the validity of the commutative proposition that
$1 + 3 = 3 + 1$.

In the diagram we are dealing with particulars, and would still be dealing
with particulars if I went on to point out that all this would apply to the

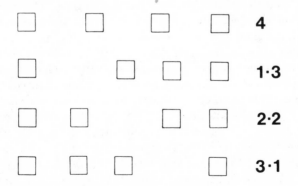

FIG. 23. Variable grouping of four objects, the top line representing
perception of one group of four; next perceived as two groups, of one and three;
next, two groups of two and two; bottom, three and one.

perception of four ferryboats or four pigeons or even, retrospectively and in imagination, the first four years of this century or the four most recent thunderstorms, and it might be thought that this is an attempt to establish the general proposition by multiplying instances—that is, by induction. That does not work. But we have seen (p. 109) that theory allows us to work with the high-level nonverbal abstraction of *something* or *anything,* and when the argument is applied to the case of four somethings or four anythings (thus, any four things), which is obviously possible in thought, theory or no theory, then the argument escapes from the limits of an inductive demonstration. The four specific blobs of Figure 23 are merely a nudge to thought, a necessary aid to the verbal communication of a logic that is not a verbal logic. We can agree that the resulting knowledge that two and two is four is not *a priori* knowledge, for it can be had only with extended experience and the resulting perceptual sophistication; but it is evidently not "merely verbal knowledge," nor empirical knowledge in the sense of a simple product of learning such as knowing that the sound of *four* is to follow the sound of *three* in counting. Instead it is one of a large and important class of psychological functions such as insight or mother love or a baby's first temper tantrum that are not learned but are yet a function of prior learning (Hebb, 1972). Knowing that two and two is four is not *a priori,* but the human being is built so that , given normal exposure to the environment, the fact must inevitably be perceived and be perceived directly.

Further consequences with respect to thought appear when we look at the process of scientific problem-solving as a form of finding the hidden figure. There is an entertainment of this kind for children ("Find the seven Indians in the picture") but there are more difficult examples, and some are difficult indeed, as Figure 24 will show most observers. (There is an element of chance in such perceptions, as there is in scientific discovery, and for a few persons the pattern hidden in Figure 24 may be seen at first glance.) In these situations the perception of the pattern is obviously a matter of segregating figure from ground, and the same is true of scientific discovery—that is, the irrelevant considerations must be separated from the relevant—but in the perceptual problem the pattern recognition occurs first and determines the segregation, and it seems clear that this must be true of scientific discovery as well. "Recognition," in the first case, is usually not recognition in a literal sense— the man in Figure 24 is not one seen before—but perception of a new member of a familiar class. This means that some items in the total picture have corresponded to and thus excited a higher-order cell-assembly combination. If this applies also to the scientific case, the discovery requires that the higher-order pattern already exists, a product of earlier experience, either singly or as a combination. The conclusion that discovery, the attainment of a new idea at maturity, always utilizes the template or templates of an earlier idea or earlier ideas, finds strong support in that pervasive use of analogy in scientific as well

FIG. 24.   Hidden figure. From Paul B. Porter, Another puzzle picture. *American Journal of Psychology*, 1954, 67, p. 550. Copyright 1954 by the Board of Trustees of the University of Illinois. By permission.

as everyday language to which I have already referred. The use becomes understandable and would be hard to account for otherwise.

It is evident that the detection of patterns in scientific data includes the case of the pattern in which something is missing, and this has its parallel in the perception of the incomplete figure, which perception nevertheless completes. In science, the completion is the postulation of an unobserved or unobservable entity or process. This way of looking at the data is of course a theory, and theory therefore is a provider of higher-order information about the array of data with which it is concerned. Perceptually, inspection of Figure 24 can provide a complete molecular knowledge of size and locus of all the patches of light of which it is composed and still leave complete ignorance of an essential property of the whole. Similarly, in science it is possible to have a full knowlege of the parts of a system and still not "understand" it—that is, be completely ignorant of the spatial and temporal patterns that it consists of at a more molar level. It is those patterns that must be perceived in one's imagination if one is to anticipate the response of the system to this treatment or that, or in the case of an active system to know what its future developments will be.

This makes it possible to define the flaw in Laplace's idea that if all were known about every particle in the universe it would be possible ideally to know all that will happen in the future, and define it succinctly. Knowing everything about those particles says nothing about the patterns they embody. That crucial lack of information is what physical, biological and social theory is about; a theory is an attempted formulation, a guess, concerning one of those patterns of existence, and knowledge of the future in Laplace's sense will be possible only when the theory of natural phenomena is complete in all respects—which is to say, never. The same flaw appears in Sir Karl Popper's (1972) idea that in a deterministic universe a physicist who had enough knowledge of the physical state of the neurons in Sir Karl's brain could have written the lecture in which he (Popper) first set forth these views, without needing to know anything about philosophy; or with the same information from Mozart's brain could have written a Mozart symphony. Knowing everything about the parts making up a complex is not to know all about the complex; the meaning of the Gestalt motto, the whole is more than the sum of its parts, is conveyed by saying that there is more information in the whole than in its parts taken singly. Here we are dealing with the inverse of the nothing-but fallacy of reductionism (p. 43), when the physiologist whose concern characteristically is with the parts of the system forgets the properties of the whole and asserts that emotion or thought is nothing but the firing of single neurons; true enough at that level of analysis, but there are other levels, and the most important knowledge about the brain—or knowledge as important as any other—can only be obtained in those more molar aspects of its function. A physicist, to follow the course of Popper's thought from a knowledge of the present state of the particles in his brain, would need a complete and sound theory of the functioning of the human brain—and that theory is about as unlikely to be available as a complete and sound theory of the universe, at least for a long, long time to come.

One more thing of great interest emerges from this drawing a parallel between thought and perception. Consider the apparently absurd idea of Mozart's that he could see as a whole, hear "in its entirety," the musical composition he had just completed mentally. The letter in which the statement was made has been regarded as of doubtful authenticity, perhaps because it seems so improbable. Yet, from the point of view at which we have arrived in our present discussion, it becomes less unintelligible, and there is another statement of undoubted authenticity that offers it complete support. I mean the statement by Henri Poincaré, in his famous lecture on the psychological processes of mathematical creativity, that he could "perceive at a glance" the course of a long and difficult piece of mathematical reasoning. The improbability of Mozart's report comes from the fact that music is sequential and cannot be heard all at once, but the transformations of mathematical reasoning are sequential too and, one would suppose, can hardly be thought all at once any more than perceived all at once. But we saw earlier in the discussion of imagery how readily one can have the illusion of an image existing like a picture "before the mind's eye" (p. 118), when it must in fact be known sequentially as far as any detail is concerned. The various parts can be "seen" at will and it readily appears that one has the whole before one and open to inspection. The image of the whole, as a higher-order cell-assembly activity, completely lacks detail, but it still is imagery of the whole and for detail there is the lower-order activity of the separate parts. The fact that Mozart's report sounds unreasonable to everday common sense is in a way evidence of authenticity, for it is so unlikely to have been thought up by one who had no such experience. The theory that makes the reports of Mozart and Poincaré intelligible in turn gains support from them.

It is possible that the special capacity of the great contributors to human knowledge is the ability to hold in mind a greater mass of detail from which to extract the relevant pattern, but all things considered this is unlikely, just as a more complete perception of detail is no help in finding the "buried" Christ in Figure 24. Rather, what one must do is somehow stand back from the detail to detect the figure. The great contributors to knowledge then are not always thinking more complex thoughts than the rest of us. Instead of learning where all the trees are, a feat of memory in detail, and deducing thence the contours of the wood, the original thinker seems first to have perceived those contours and from this to have been able to see where the trees must be: intellectually a less laborious task, and for that matter, less difficult later, for those who are able to see that larger pattern once it is pointed out. It is worth quoting Poincaré at length in this respect. After denying that he has a good memory, even with respect to mathematics, he goes on to say (Ghiselin, 1955):

> Why does [memory] not fail me in a difficult piece of mathematical reasoning...? Evidently because it is guided by the general march of the reasoning. A mathematical demonstration is not a simple juxtaposition of syllogisms, it is syllogisms *placed in a certain order,* and the order in which these elements are placed is much more important than the elements themselves. If I have the feeling, the intuition, so to speak, of this order, so as to perceive at a glance the reasoning as a whole, I need no longer fear lest I forget one of the elements, for each of them will take its allotted place in the array, and that without any effort of memory on my part.
>
> It seems to me then, in repeating a reasoning learned, that I could have invented it. This is often only an illusion; but even then, even if I am not so gifted as to create it by myself, I myself reinvent it in so far as I repeat it [p.34-35].

In the same way, one might almost say, one reinvents the evidence for the germ theory of disease or the theory of evolution whenever one has occasion to think about it—it is clear at least that, just as "the march of the reasoning" kept Poincaré on the track and freed him of a burden of memory, so a general theory serves to organize a great number of empirical facts and aid in their recall. Difficult as some modern theories may be, for those of us who have no eye for the forest of physics, or molecular genetics, or biochemistry, or economics (or even psychology), it is evident that the effect of theory for the initiate in any of these fields is primarily simplifying. At some early stage in the course of discovery, then, the innovator sees a simpler picture. Laborious and prolonged as the testing and demonstration of a new theoretical conception must be, these complications in general must follow rather than precede discovery.

THE THEORY OF HYPNOSIS

A new dimension in the experimental study of thought was added by Hilgard's *Divided Consciousness* (1977). The book describes the discovery of two separate consciousness, different states of awareness, in certain hypnotized subjects, and the ability of the hypnotist to communicate with either consciousness at will. The discovery is of first importance for cognitive psychology in general, and of special interest here because of a possible relation to certain features of cognitive learning considered in the preceding chapter.

Hypnosis has been a standing reminder that all is not well with the theory of thought, for it—hypnosis—has entirely lacked explanation. Obviously important, close to the heart of things (in view of the profound changes it can make, at least temporarily, in the subject's relation to his or her environment), it still lacked any connection with the theories of perception and learning and so on that make up cognitive psychology. A connection with suggestibility, yes, but what is suggestibility but a first step toward hypnosis? To explain the one by the other is to beg the question. Now Hilgard has gone far to break down the wall between hypnosis and cognitive psychology by providing new and powerful evidence of a dissociation in hypnosis that can be related to features of common experience. Instead of a deeply mysterious state almost reminding one of witchcraft, hypnosis in Hilgard's hands simply becomes a more extreme form of such a duality of thought as that referred to earlier, when one reads *Little Red Ridinghood* aloud at bedtime while wondering how long it will take the child to get asleep and let one get back to the evening paper or, while lecturing to a class or telling a joke, *listening* to what is being said to see whether lecture or joke is going over well.

There is a certain drama about Hilgard's discovery. He was giving a classroom demonstration of hypnosis and suggestibility, using an experienced subject who as it happened was blind (thus when he became deaf in the demonstration he was very much cut off from his surroundings). The subject was hypnotized and told that on the count of three he would become deaf but would be able to hear whenever a hand was placed on his shoulder.

Hilgard counted to three, then showed the class that the subject was now unresponsive to sudden loud sounds as well as to questions or comment. However, a member of the class asked whether it was not possible that some part of the subject might still be able to hear. Hilgard acted on the suggestion, apparently just to show that there was nothing in it. Speaking quietly, he said to the hypnotized subject that some things happening in the nervous system are not part of one's awareness; if there was some part of the subject that had been hearing during the preceding tests, he asked it to raise a forefinger. "To the surprise of the instructor, as well as the class," the finger rose.

This was the moment of discovery, and Hilgard went on to complete discovery by showing that the subject was still deaf, had heard nothing, but was puzzled to feel his finger rise without intending it. Hilgard momentarily restored hearing, promised an explanation later, but asked the subject in the meantime to report what had happened so far. The subject recalled being told that he would become deaf on the count of three, and that Hilgard had counted to three. Then everything became quiet. This was boring, so he started to think about a statistical problem he was interested in. Without warning he felt his forefinger rise—which he would now like explained. Allowing the subject to become deaf again by removing his hand from his shoulder, Hilgard now addressed the "other part" that had heard him before and had responded by raising a finger, and asked *him* for a report. It turned out that this other part, to whom or to which Hilgard refers as the "hidden observer," was aware of all that had gone on and could report it.

When it was looked for in other subjects under hypnosis, the same dissociation of separate states of awareness was found in about half of a group high in hypnotic susceptibility. Here hypnotic analgesia has a special interest. The hypnotized subject is told that he or she will feel no pain when the left hand and forearm are held in circulating ice-water. In those cases in which dissociation is found, the subject denies feeling pain, or much pain, but at the same time the hidden observer reports pain at almost the intensity that is experienced when not under hypnosis. This report could be made by word of mouth, but Hilgard then turned to automatic writing by the right hand or to a method of key-pressing as the means of communication.

As soon as one tries to talk about these surprising results one faces a problem of terminology. New concepts are needed. Hilgard uses the term hidden observer as a metaphor only. As such it conveys well the idea of the passive role (passive, but well-informed) of the hitherto unsuspected co-conscious, but it may also lead to thinking of that segment as possibly a more complete or more self-sufficient consciousness—more nearly a separate mind—than perhaps it is. Sperry's and Gazzaniga's split-brain patients have made us used to the idea of two minds in one head, but the parallel with the hypnotic dissociation is not really close. There is for example no question of separate anatomical loci for the dissociated activities—let me call them

Consciousness A and Consciousness B—in left and right hemispheres; for Consciousness B (the nondominant hidden observer) can in favorable circumstances acquire control of the speech apparatus of the left hemisphere in order to talk. What Hilgard describes is a subtler, more fluid relation than an anatomical separation would permit.

There is an unexpected convergence of these results of Hilgard's with a problem of cognitive learning discussed earlier (p. 102). The problem was to account for the prompt, constantly occurring, one-trial incidental learning of everyday life. It was proposed that this can be understood if well-organized cell-assembly groups when excited together tend to "cohere" temporarily, so that exciting one excites the other. For this there is physiological warrant of a sort. The crossing of a synapse by the impulse leaves the synapse more readily traversible thereafter, with a short-term memory effect (longer-lasting change requires multiple crossings of the synapse). There is this much psychological warrant also, that no other explanation has been provided for this much disregarded but actually commonest form of adult human learning.

It may now be proposed that what happens in hypnosis is the massive coherence of cell-assemblies in a pattern set up by the spoken words of the hypnotist, the repetitive verbal formulation tending to reduce the normal variability of assembly combinations; that on some occasions and in some subjects this alignment may go much further than on others; and that in some subjects there is coherence in two groups instead of one—Consciousness A and Consciousness B. This is all speculation, and even if there is something in it the details will take long to work out. The exciting thing is that Hilgard has made possible a physiologically intelligible idea of the nature of hypnosis. The hypothesis implies that with repeated trials, with repetition of the same alignment of assemblies, the synaptic modification will become less temporary. The alignment then will be easier or quicker established, which of course accords with the experimental facts of hypnosis.

It might seem that to account for the separation of the two blocs of assemblies in the case of dissociation, as well as for the denial of pain, a massive cortical inhibition is required. This does not really follow. True, there must be inhibition at the level of cord and brain stem, when reflex responsiveness to pain stimuli is suppressed, but things are different at a more cognitive level. The theory proposes that the same neurons must enter into different assemblies. Then the mere existence of assembly X could be enough to prevent the establishment of assembly Y, for the period of X's duration. No inhibition of Y would be needed. In the same way, if what we ordinarily think of as an idea is a complex of assemblies, the existence of one idea will preclude the existence of certain other ideas in which some of the same components enter. As for pain, we have already seen that it is a complex, made up both of the simple perception of the occurrence of a noxious event and of an emotional reaction. It is conceivable that the effect of the hypnotist's instruction to feel no pain blocks both perception and emotional reaction by preempting essential components of both mental processes. And further, when Consciousness B indicates that he, she or it knows that pain is present, this, as I read Hilgard's words, sounds like a report of the sensory event only—as if the emotional component was blocked as much for Consciousness B, the hidden observer, as for the dominant Consciousness A. This then is not plausible by means of inhibition.

All this calls into question some well-established notions about what is conscious and what is not, such as the concept of subliminal perception that supposes that something can be perceived but at the same time not be conscious. We are accustomed to think of any mental process that cannot be recalled and reported as subconscious or unconscious. Now, when one of Hilgard's special subjects is questioned after hypnosis and knows nothing of the hidden observer or its activity, are we to say that that activity was unconscious? No, for what Hilgard is telling us is that it was fully conscious, but in a separate stream of thought. What is unreportable now, therefore, was not necessarily unconscious earlier. Even in more ordinary circumstances, thought may be unreportable only because recall is impossible, even seconds later, because it would need the reinstatement of the whole context of earlier activity of which the thought was part.

From this point of view one must now question all that talk about creativity by the unconscious, with the implication that the process was something other than the processes of the normal conscious thought. When Housman suddenly and mysteriously found himself aware of part of a new poem, ready for him to do some work himself and complete it, or when Poincaré was surprised to know the answer to a mathematical question that—apparently— he had not been asking, the poem or the mathematical idea is supposed to have been achieved in a separate realm, the unconscious, apparently by some other means than rational thought. But what are the facts? All we know for sure—all that Housman or Poincaré knew for sure—is that neither of them recalled any prior mental activity, only the end product. In effect, then, we may be dealing here with a failure of memory only. Consequently, there is nothing here to justify the quite radical conclusion that there are different *kinds* of creative mental activities. Instead we can recognize the fact that separate streams of thought do exist apart from hypnosis, with the possibility that on occasion the cues of one stream of thought may be insufficient to reinstate and thus make reportable the content of the other.

9
Scientific Law in Human Thought

This chapter is concerned with law and order in the world of thought; with the idea that the external world is orderly and that prediction can be made reliably, as well as the idea that the same rules apply to human behavior.

I expect to show that the classic problem of prediction is not what it seems to be. The problem was posed by David Hume in 1739, pointing out that one cannot be certain that something will happen in the future simply because it has always happened that way in the past. It has appeared that such a view is denied by the success of scientific law, and by the fact that scientists do predict successfully. In fact, however, there is no necessity about scientific prediction. The unforeseen conceivably may intervene at any point.

On the other hand, it appears that the universe must be an orderly one in human thought, for determinism can be shown to be logically inescapable. Free will, a biologically evident fact in the behavior of the higher animal, is not denied by that proposition; but ESP at best becomes highly improbable.

SCIENTIFIC LAW AND PREDICTION

There are two kinds of scientific law, one of which is a rule of thought rather than a summary of observed events, the other essentially inductive. The first is exemplified by the laws of motion and of thermodynamics. A law of this kind is empty of empirical content, makes no real prediction, and may be regarded by the logician as not really a law but a disguised definition of one of its terms (e.g., failure of the first law of motion, as we will see, indicates the presence of some "external force" such as friction). However, for the scientist this kind of law is the truly fundamental one. The second kind is exemplified by Kepler's first law, that planetary orbits about the sun are ellipses, or in psychology by the Weber-Fechner law, that sensory intensity increases as the logarithm of stimulus intensity. A law of this kind certainly makes a prediction—and therefore, unlike the first kind, is falsifiable. Because it is more fundamental in the scientist's thought, and just because it cannot be falsified by discovering a contrary example, we may regard the first kind as the true scientific law. It constitutes a peculiarity of scientific thought that is a main concern of this chapter.

The first of Newton's three laws of motion (this one in fact discovered by Galileo) says that a body at rest will continue at rest, a body in motion will continue in uniform motion in a straight line, unless acted on by an external force. This law is regarded as absolutely valid, but it does not refer to anything that has ever been observed; the motion of this planet means that no one has observed an object at rest (a meaningless conception anyway, now that Newton's absolute space has been done away with), and as for motion unaffected by an external force, the law of gravitation means that an external force is always present so this cannot be observed either. Since it does not describe anything that happens, the law makes no prediction and cannot be tested experimentally. When some approximation to its conditions has been achieved (for example, a billiard ball rolling on a smooth level surface) and what the law calls for does not happen (instead of continuing to roll, the ball slows down and stops) this is not treated as evidence that the law is wrong but as evidence of the presence of an external force (in this case friction, even if there is no other way in which the friction of a rolling ball on a polished surface can be detected).

Similarly with the law of conservation of energy: The law says that a perpetual-motion machine is impossible, but if something seemed to show perpetual motion it would not disprove the law but would mean that there was some unknown source of energy present.

To all intents and purposes, so far, the sun has been a perpetual-motion machine, its tremendous unending outpouring of energy being terribly puzzling in the past to the physicist. Energy cannot be created (or destroyed), so where was the heat coming from? Now by virtue of Einstein's $E = MC^2$ (energy = mass × the square of the speed of light), it is understood that the sun's matter is being turned directly into energy and—since C in that equation is a very large number—a little matter goes a long way. The sun can be expected to continue for some time yet, but the explanation means it will run down eventually. Therefore, the sun is not really a perpetual-motion machine but merely one that is taking a long time to use up its reserve.

Kepler's law of elliptical planetary orbits on the other hand was quite different. It was essentially inductive and empirical, described and predicted real events, and was quite open to disproof whenever real events did not conform. Thus there is no necessity about what it predicts. If the planets have always moved in ellipses, according to the available data, it does not follow that they always will. Kepler's ellipse soon turned out to be only an approximation, and the more fundamental Newtonian laws that explained the elliptical orbits also said that they could not be perfect because of the gravitational influence between planets. And Newton's laws said further that if, by some disastrous chance, another sun-sized body should enter the system the present orbits would be completely disrupted. Since things could happen that would change the pattern it described, Kepler's general statement has limits as a prediction. (A statement about the ideal case of the sun and one planet, undisturbed by others, would be different matter.) Any cosmologist would agree that the near regularity of past planetary behavior cannot guarantee continuance in the future, which agrees with Hume's position.

However, that case—dependent on the intrusion of a disturbing factor—may seem to the reader not to be what Hume was talking about. His principle is tacitly amended to mean that a past regularity cannot be depended on even when nothing has been changed. Whether he thought this I do not know, but he did not say it. The point is crucial and it leads to a significant feature of our knowledge of the real world.

Take a different example, the electrical conductivity of copper that certain philosophers have already discussed. I have a piece of copper wire, let us say, that I have tested and repeatedly found to conduct electricity with low resistance. I know also from the books that copper has always been found to be a good conductor. What conclusion can I draw from these facts, logically? There is no necessary basis for supposing that this piece of wire, put into a circuit with an ammeter, will give the same result as before; but I may still with full assurance assert that *copper* will conduct electricity as in the past, for if this wire is now nonconductive something has changed it and it is no longer copper. Electrical conductivity is part of the "definition" of copper, a means of identifying it, along with a specific gravity of 8.9, a reddish color, and certain other physical as well as chemical properties. If this particular piece of matter is no longer conductive it has been changed by some agency, hitherto unknown but now detectable whenever that change is observed. The probability of such an occurrence is low but it cannot be assumed to be zero, in view of the occasions in the history of science when departures from expectation have led to the discovery of new entities or new properties of known entities.

What this says is that there is nothing in science that means the necessary occurrence of any specific event. Scientific laws and such general propositions as that copper conducts electricity do not predict in quite the way they seem to. We must distinguish between (A) the necessary truth of one of these propositions in a theoretical universe and (B) the necessity of any specific event, however confidently the latter may be predicted. The chemist has no doubt that an explosion will result from putting a match to a mixture of hydrogen and oxygen, and here he is on solid ground; but he cannot be absolutely and finally certain before the event that he is dealing with hydrogen, for example, or that no new variable will enter the next test to interfere with the union of H_2 and O_2 and modify the result. Even though no one knows of any way in which stored hydrogen might change, or any variable that could affect the combustion in some other manner, *there is no possible way, logically, to prove the nonexistence of such a thing,* to be encountered in the future. There is no basis consequently for dogmatic insistence on the inevitability of any outcome of a scientific procedure, or even on the continued appearance of the regularities of nature that are familiar to us.

To clarify this it will be worth while looking at an actual example. In 1890 there was a well-established regularity between atomic weight and chemical properties. Each substance had its own atomic weight and its own distinctive way of reacting to the presence of other substances. It was therefore very puzzling for Rayleigh to discover that nitrogen extracted from the air weighed more than nitrogen prepared from one of its compounds and yet, with exhaustive tests, to find no evidence of any chemical difference between them (i. e., evidence of an impurity). In both cases, apparently, nothing but nitrogen was present, but chemists were forced to the conclusion that the atmosphere must contain a small proportion of some heavier gas, hitherto unknown and unsuspected. Unlikely as it seemed, the gas could have no chemical properties—and so it turned out, in the later discovery by Ramsay of the inert gases, so called because it seemed for long that they were inactive chemically; argon, helium, neon, krypton, and xenon.

Here we have the operation of two tacitly accepted principles. One of them, that the same thing could not now have one weight, now another, remained inviolable; therefore, nitrogen from the air must contain some impurity. The other principle was that a difference of weight meant a difference of chemical properties. The first of these is essentially definitional—if something has a different weight, it is not the same substance—and so was inviolable, but the second was inductive and related two independently identifiable entities. It could therefore be refuted, and was.

Thus the inert gases were the same chemically despite their different weights—although the "sameness" was only a complete lack of chemical properties (which destroyed another principle, that any substance must have chemical properties). But the disease soon went further. The inert gases were alike only in a negative sense. The isotopes discovered by Soddy and others about 1911 made it possible for substances with the same positive chemical properties to differ in weight. Carbon 12, carbon 13, and carbon 14, for example, act alike chemically though they have different weights; and nitrogen 14, almost identical in weight with carbon 14, is very different from it chemically. These results were indeed disturbing to thought in physical science and were part of a Kuhnian revolution, but they were not offensive to the scientific method itself, for the empirical generalizations they upset were seen in retrospect to have no real necessity about them.

DETERMINISM: LOGICALLY INESCAPABLE

There are certain conclusions to be drawn from this line of thought, concerning determinism and the question of order in the universe. It may seem from what has been said that science does not find order but imposes it, by formulating so-called laws and assuming constancy in nature ("copper always conducts electricity," "nitrogen always has the same weight") and then, when nature acts otherwise, inventing some new entity to save appearances.

This does happen, but, in a developed science, not often. The scientist is much more likely to look for errors of measurement, or of observation, or of interpretation. I am told for example that there was a chemist who devoted his career to determining the true atomic weight of lead; getting different values from different samples, he did not postulate different kinds of lead as he might have (and would have been correct in doing so) but persisted in looking for a single nonexistent true value; there are several isotopes of lead, and different samples give different answers. Unobserved and unobservable entities are not readily postulated, and even when postulated and widely accepted may later be discarded. Phlogiston, caloric, and the luminiferous ether are examples. Phrenological localizations, spontaneous generation, and preformation of the embryo may belong here also. But one principle is retained, though tacitly: Namely, the same thing has the same properties, the same situation the same upshot.

Now this is the principle of determinism, and determinism is something that both scientist and philosopher are apt to be skittish about. In scientific *practice* it is taken for granted even by scientists who disclaim it when talking philosophy. The reason for a disclaimer may be that determinism in the physical sciences means determinism in human behavior, and this is thought—mistakenly—to deprive man of free will.

The situation I have described leaves the scientist no choice. He must be a determinist if there is to be consistency in his thought. As I considered this aspect of scientific method, when first drafting a statement of this argument, I realized that the argument must be more general. It applies to any human thought, including the philosopher's, and leads to the conclusion that determinism is logically inescapable. I am aware of all the argument to the contrary, and realize that my own argument may have a flaw. Nevertheless, I do not find the flaw, and it now appears to me that those who abjure determinism do so not on logical grounds but on grounds of taste—a dislike for the idea that all is preordained—or, as mentioned previously, because they think that determinism rules out free will. Having first made up their minds, they then look for rational support.

The situation is this. If scientist or engineer can make certain identification of a substance only by its response to test, by its reaction to external agencies and forces, then there is no way in which he can find the same substance behaving now in one way, now in another; for if it does not behave in the same way it is not the same substance. As we have seen, the copper we know must conduct electricity; otherwise, it is not copper (or not the same *kind* of copper). In the same way, if the nature and components of a given situation can be identified with certainty only by the outcome—the result of its own activity or the result of scientific test—there is no way in which it can be said that the same situation can have a variable outcome. It is important to observe that sameness—or lack of change—cannot be guaranteed by protecting the components of the situation from external influence, for the situation may already have within it the seeds of change, undetected, and, also, we can only protect against the external influences we know about already. Faraday in 1833 had no possibility of protecting his Leyden jars against cosmic rays, Rayleigh had no way of thinking that the nitrogen he was isolating from the air was already contaminated. The continued sameness of a substance cannot be guaranteed by its having remained untouched on the chemist's shelf or by being held continuously in the hand. It can only be known by retesting.

Evidently this argument does not apply only in science and technology. The identity of any object of everyday experience is determined by test and by its behavior in common situations. The "test" that is applied is usually a sensory test, looking, listening, touching, smelling or tasting, and the result is the perception of color, the quality of sound, and so on, but there may be of course more strenuous tests of bending or breaking or chewing. To identify an object is then to state a theory of its future properties for the perceiver, and of its future behavior in certain situations. Naming a stone as such says that it is cold in cool weather but retains heat, resists strong pressure, is heavy in the hand, will lie still on the ground when the wind blows. A companion's friendliness is known as a theory based on certain forms of behavior, including response to such tests as saying "Hello" or asking for a cigarette. The test may fail and give evidence that something has changed. The other may be still friendly (theory can still stand) but in a temporary state of annoyance or preoccupation. Only later tests will determine whether this is so. The identification of friendliness is evidently complicated compared to that of stoniness, but they are alike in each depending on the presence of certain diagnostic signs. If those signs change—if the stone can now be moved by a puff of wind or the friend continues unresponsive—the stone or the person, or the situation in which the test is made, has changed. The same object or the same situation must behave in the same way, for that is the only way in which it can be known to be the same. This is determinism. It consists essentially of saying that A is A and not *not-A*. There is no logical alternative.

Now it is true that there are scientists and philosophers who have talked as if indeterminism were a matter of fact—not merely a philosophic presupposition but experimentally established fact—at the subatomic level. For example, Reichenbach (1951) has spoken of Heisenberg's uncertainty principle as proof of a lack of causality. But this would be proof of the null hypothesis, which is not possible; there is no way in which such an absence of underlying order could be established even when it is agreed, on fundamental theoretical grounds, that *prediction* is impossible. As for the physicist who declares for indeterminism, he is talking philosophy and his views should be evaluated on that ground. Instead of asking him for his opinion, one can look to see what he does in his theoretical and experimental research, and by that test he will be found to be a determinist. The atom does not provide support for indeterminism.

What I have discussed here is a rule of thought, an apparent logical necessity about the meaning of the concept of *same,* but also one that implies lawfulness—order and regularity—in the universe. One might ask, therefore (as others have asked), whether that implication is correct. The answer might be another question: What meaning can lawfulness have for the human thinker, except that general conformity with expectation in common experience that we all know? Stones fall, smoke rises, spring follows winter, cats meow generation after generation, seeds sprout, and so forth. But a simpler answer is that conformity to law is a hypothesis, justified by results to an overwhelming degree and therefore to be held true until disproved.

How might it be disproved? It is evidently not possible to do so. We have no way of being certain that even in a lawful universe the regularities as we know them will continue, for some existing entity still unknown may intervene— even in an orderly world there is no reason to think that we know all—or some emergent process, hitherto innocent, may reach a critical and destructive stage with no departure from lawfulness. So the universe may be fully lawful and orderly and still present us with a disastrously different situation tomorrow. Although we have no reason to think such a development will occur, no one can be certain that the air of this planet will continue to be breathable, nor that rain will continue its intermittent appearance in the temperate zones—nor that another ice age is not imminent. The sun, it is thought, will not become a nova, but what certainty can that opinion have? Or the sun may begin to run out of fuel and become too cool to support life at such a distance. We cannot be certain. But such possibilities still do not deny the existence of natural law.

FREE WILL: A BIOLOGICAL PHENOMENON

There are those who deny the existence of free will in man because it would be inconsistent with natural law, and those who reject law, or determinism, for the same reason. Both are wrong. Free will does exist, and it is fully compatible with, and indeed a product of, the operation of natural law: in an effect known as evolution.

The simple elementary meaning of free will, or volition, is being able to do what you want to do (or decide to do, whether you "want" to or not) instead of being compelled to act or not act by circumstances. This says clearly that free will is control of behavior by thought. It is therefore not peculiar to man since (as we saw in Chapter 4) thought can be detected even in the lower mammals and is quite evident in monkey and ape. We are inclined to recognize it in human beings when there is some question of a moral choice, but it is also evident when a hungry man saves seeds for planting or a pigheaded one persists in carrying out some unlikely scheme despite discouragement—or when a chimpanzee carries out a planned and deceitful attack. None of this implies indeterminism unless thought itself is indeterministic.

There is always some unpredictability about voluntary behavior, but this is fully accounted for by the complexity of knowing, by any conceivable means, what the present state is of each of the billions of neurons in the human brain and therefore what they will be doing in the future. But the activity of the individual neuron is highly predictable, and shows no sign of departure from the known laws of physics and chemistry. The biologically evident phenomenon of free will, the control of behavior at least some of the time by the thought process, thus provides no more evidence in support of indeterminism than Heisenberg's uncertainty principle, which says only that the momentum of a particle and its position cannot both be determined, though either may be singly.

It is evident that when determinism and the uniformity of natural law are denied it is usually because of distaste for what may seem to be their consequences. Even Popper (1972) rejects physical determinism because it would be a "nightmare," and he then must find (unconvincing) reasons in support of that position. Being a dualist, he sees that an immaterial mind cannot affect a material brain unless there is some play, some possibility of slippage, in the operation, for example, of the law of conservation of energy; he therefore rejects lawfulness. He might instead have rejected interactionism, but he would still apparently be left with the view that determinsm would make man an automaton with no power of choice and no creativity since, Popper says, nothing new is possible when all has been determined at the beginning. This last is in connection with the surprising idea (surprising from

Popper especially) that in a deterministic universe a physicist ignorant of music could still write a Mozart symphony if he had full information about the cells of Mozart's brain and body; as we have seen (p. 126) this is wrong *in principle,* lacking a final and complete theory of thought, even for a demonic physicist capable of knowing and keeping in mind simultaneously all the "precise physical states" of a human body. (What determinism *does* imply is that if the physicist could arrange to duplicate Mozart's adult brain exactly and expose it to the same sensory and nutritive influences, the symphonies would be written again; but that is a different proposition.) Again, the idea that there would be no choice: In the context of determinism choice has a different look about it, but it still exists.

If it is predetermined that I will take the left-hand turning at a fork in my path, it is also predetermined that this will be preceded by a certain activity in my brain, causally related to my behavior, and that activity is *choice.* Even in a deterministic universe, the living higher animal is not in any sense an automaton, for an automaton's mechanism remains the same from one time to the next and in the same situation does the same thing. Though the cells that compose the human body, and especially the human brain, can plausibly be regarded as automata, the whole organism can not, for the brain is never the same twice running. It is modified by every experience, an effect that we call memory. The pattern of its activity is continually changing, deterministically or not, and saying that if there is predetermination there are no new patterns—the essential meaning of creativity—is to use the word *new* in a very peculiar sense.

I can see no way in which determinism lowers the worth and dignity of human beings.

EXTRASENSORY PERCEPTION: A PROBLEM

ESP constitutes a problem for the good reason that all our present knowledge of the physical world and of the physiology of the human body make telepathy extremely unlikely and clairvoyance impossible, but at the same time there are certain experiences that may seem to admit of no other explanation. There is also a body of experimental reports to support the latter view. The result is a difficult choice if we are to lay any claim to consistency of thought. Either the experimental data are untrustworthy and those apparent cases of ESP outside the laboratory are not what they seem—that is, we must reject ESP completely—or we must recognize that an extensive revision of physics and physiology is being called for.

It is not inconceivable that telepathy exists. Telepathy is the direct communication of one mind with another, bypassing sensory channels, and might be thought of as an effect of the electrical activity of one brain on the neurons of a second brain. This is inconsistent with anything we know about the physiology of cortical function—the transmission must have a blanket effect of the whole receiving brain, which possibly might have a general exciting action or a depressing one, but hardly the selective action on particular neurons required to produce an image or a train of ideas—but it cannot be dogmatically ruled out, on principle. Also, it seems that telepathy is unaffected by distance, whereas the effect of electrical potentials must diminish as the square of the distance. However, it is conceivable that somehow there is such an effect. It is extremely unlikely in the light of present knowledge, but present knowledge is limited.

Clairvoyance is even more of a problem. It is a direct nonsensory awareness not of the content of another person's mind, but of something inert. It is like being able to read the numbers of a pack of cards that is out of sight. Unlike another person's brain, which is active electrically, the cards are inert—as far as we know. Unless there is some form of energy being transmitted by them, reading what is on them seems impossible. That is, clairvoyance seems impossible. We can leave aside psychokinesis and precognition as quite inconsistent with current scientific knowledge (to say the least of what might be said) and still have, in telepathy and even more in clairvoyance, a set of reported phenomena whose existence would require a thoroughgoing revision of physical and physiological science. Either physics and physiology are way off the beam, or there are flaws in the evidence of parapsychology.

That evidence is of two kinds: (1) from laboratory experiment, and (2) from a kind of experience outside the laboratory that may strike at any time and be very convincing to the person concerned.

1.   The earlier experimental evidence was reviewed by Hansel (1966) and his criticism is now strongly reinforced by Diaconis (1978). The systematic and reliable results that would be needed to settle a matter of such magnitude do not exist. ESP is not a minor matter, nor a by-way apart from other scientific questions where one can indulge one's imagination without reckoning the cost, which is what the parapsychologist seems to attempt—at least, I see no discussion of mechanisms or of the significance that positive results must have for other fields of science. From this broader point of view the evidence falls far short of conviction. There are still the twin problems of fraud and of self-deception. Fraud does occur. Experimental methods still tend to be inadequate, and the experimental controls are less satisfactory than one might suppose in reading the published reports. Making that point, based on his detailed first or second-hand knowledge of the course of events in some 30-odd experiments, Diaconis (1978) says: "In every case, the details of what actually [happened] prevent the experiment from being seriously considered

as evidence for paranormal phenomena" (p. 136). If ESP exists it must revolutionize physical and biological science. The existing evidence does not yet require us to take such a step.

2.   There is a different kind of evidence in certain individual experiences that may be as unexpected as a bolt of lightning or an earthquake—and equally convincing to the person concerned. For example, a woman whose husband is away on a business trip wakes in the night feeling that he is in trouble; when he gets back home two or three days later he tells her about a near escape from a car accident, about at the time that she woke up and worried. Or a son suddenly feels anxious about his aged mother, living in another town, and then gets a letter saying that she fell and broke her hip, as elderly women do. A great number of such cases have been recorded since the 19th-century founding of the Society for Psychical Research, and a representative selection can be found in Gardner Murphy's (1961) *Challenge of Psychical Research.*

How are we to regard such evidence? The answer of the skeptic is that it all is coincidence, but this does not convince the person who has had such an experience. For him the coincidence is altogethere too coincidental. I have known personally two people to whom such a thing has happened; one was inclined toward ESP anyway, but the other was a physical scientist who was shaken by it. He was very disturbed by an apparent need to revise his whole way of thinking about the nature of existence. I must say that my argument, opposing the conclusion on a statistical basis, did not seem very convincing at the time.

But there *is* a statistical argument. The objection to the explanation by coincidence is that it is too improbable, and how does one assess the degree of probability? We do not know, for example, how many people of the two-hundred-odd million in the United States are worrying at any one time about the welfare of an absent relative. Certainly no record is kept when the fear later turns out to be groundless, but let us try some assumptions. Suppose that the number of persons with relatives of whom they are fond but who are at a distance is one percent or less of the adult population—say a total of one million. Suppose that the number of these who spontaneously have an attack of worry about the absent relative is also one per cent. Now the number is down to ten thousand. The relative being worried about is likely to be engaged in a hazardous occupation, like driving on the highway; or old and subject to accident, like falling in the bathtub; or subject to illness, like a heart attack. Suppose then, finally, that one-tenth of one per cent of these have an accident or near escape or an attack *at about the same time* as the other's spontaneous feeling of concern, and the result will be ten cases that might be reported to the American Society for Psychical Research as clear evidence of telepathy.

I say "about the same time" because the reports of telepathy almost always involve memory, and memory is fallible. It loses detail, as we all know, but it is also apt to modify the detail that is retained. The case for telepathy assumes that the memory of an earlier premonition, after one learns of the illness or accident of the absent relative, can be relied on, but it is possible that receiving the news can change memory subtly, so that the promonition becomes sharper in corresponding detail, and corresponds better in time ("*That must have been* just when I woke up thinking of mother . . ."). In saying so I do not impugn the good faith of those who report such experiences, for such changes of memory do occur, and I have moreover an experience of my own that on a more mundane level may be an example of the same thing.

I am a player of various games of solitaire and, watching the run of the cards as I lay them down in the tableau, I have on a number of occasions thought, If this next card is a deuce of spades (for example), such and such could be done with the cards—and lo and behold, the deuce is the next card. The experience is not infrequent, and it is such as to make me, at times, stop and seriously consider what is going on. The impulse to see more than chance causation is very strong.

Here we know something of the probabilities. The chance of being right, *by chance,* is one in less than 52 (since some of the 52 cards of the pack are already exposed). Let us say that it is, in a particular case, one in 40. Then, as in the argument above, if I make such guesses as many as 40 times I can expect to be right once. Having watched myself with this in mind I know that I do make guesses—but: enough to account for the number of hits? I cannot tell, for there is a problem of remembering the guesses that do not pay off, and this draws attention to the second point. It is likely that the confirmation of a guess changes one's memory of the guess—a passing thought of the deuce of spades becomes something very different as one recalls it after the card actually appears. I cannot be certain that this is so; perhaps I have clairvoyance; but the probability still is that all such evidence amounts to a fallacy of observation instead of a factual basis for overturning physics, neurophysiology and the law of the conservation of mass-energy.

10 A World of Thought

The world the scientist deals with is in large part an imagined world, not perceived, and some of the peculiarities of scientific thought are more intelligible when this is kept in mind. The layman also lives in a world of the imagination, which helps to account for much of his activity, but the case of the scientist is more interesting because of the contrast between his persistent emphasis on sticking to data, to observable fact, and the way in which in practice he uses his data as launching pad for taking off into the unknown and the unobservable. The data are essential but in general the things he is really interested in are things that he must know in imagination only, features of a world of thought and not perceived.

THE LARGE AND THE SMALL

It is easy to recognize that situation in the case of the physicist whose submicroscopic particles and nuclear interactions can never be directly observed. They must be known by inference, as theoretical entities and processes. But it is not only the very small that must be known in such a way; it is also true of the very large, such as a weather system spread over half a continent, or the continent itself. One can see and feel a rain storm, as part of the system, but no one perceives the larger patterns of rain and wind that determine the behavior of the whole. To know the system the meteorologist must combine the reports of a hundred or five hundred observers; even if he is provided also with a television display from a satellite, showing the system as a whole, the internal detail is missing from which to know what is going on and perhaps what will be going on tomorrow. The data come piecemeal; the whole must be constructed in thought.

Again, to know a continent: Those of us who live in North America see it every day, in part, but what we see tells us as little about it as feeling rain in one's face would tell one about the extent and pattern of a summer storm. A new way of observing North America has become possible in this latter half of the 20th century, so there are people who have actually seen it as a whole from a space capsule, but, as with a weather system, this is at the cost of losing essential detail. The scars of past glaciations, the fossil record, the layers of sediment from the great inland sea, the earthquake and volcanic record and all the evidence from which to conclude that the western mountain ranges are a continuing result of friction between North American and Pacific tectonic plates—these are necessary features of the scientific conception of the continent. "North America," as a scientific entity, is an imaginative construct. The reality is there, but it is a reality with molar properties that are not known by observation but must be found in the masses of molecular data that the human eye *can* observe and report.

In biological and social science the situation is much the same. One can see the part products of an evolutionary process—members of a species—one at a time, but the process itself is not observable, nor the species as a whole with its characteristic internal variability. A species is a statistical artifact, known only in thought. The sociologist or social psychologist studying groups can rarely see a group as a whole, and when he does, cannot observe its internal relations or their course of development, except as a set of isolated incidents. The three-dimensional motion picture he is interested in, the temporal reality, must be known from a set of stills.

In all these cases it is reasonable to object that the things being investigated do after all exist; the investigator is perhaps not as fanciful as this makes him appear, since in each case there is an objective reality that corresponds to the conceptual structure. However, there is more to consider. Look next at cases in which science gives serious consideration to things that are known not to exist.

CONCERN WITH THE NONEXISTENT

We saw in the preceding chapter how the first law of motion, a cornerstone of physical science, concerns the regularity of occurrence of something that has never occurred and never can, except in imagination. The ideal liquid and the ideal gas are imagination also; Conant (1951) has pointed out that "an apparently self-evident proposition in hydrostatics turns out to be true only for a liquid that does not in fact exist," and it may be added that this liquid is the one referred to in existing theory and the one that students are taught about.

Another example comes from the determination of the significance or nonsignificance of a difference, in experimental tests, and the probable error of measurement. In both cases a careful statistical analysis is made of a population known not to exist. The purpose is entirely serious—not to promote some theoretical fantasy but the opposite, to keep experimenters down to earth and help them avoid unjustified conclusions.

Consider the experiment from which it was concluded that the early environment affects adult intelligence (p. 94). Two groups of rats were reared in ways that had never been done before, one in an enriched environment, one in a deprived environment. In a rat-intelligence test at maturity the first group made an average of 137 errors, the second group an average of 234 errors. The free-environment rats did better, but—was the difference "significant," or could this be a chance result? Might the result come out the other way if the experiment were done over again with new groups? Fundamentally, the question was whether the same difference would be found as often as the test was made, and statisticians have taught us to put the question this way: Regard the scores of the two groups of rats as samples from the same infinitely large population, and then determine how often two samples as different as these would be drawn at random (as one might deal two hands from an infinitely large pack of cards). If there could be no population from which two such different samples would be obtained as often as 5% of the time, the difference is said to be significant at the 5% level: In other words, the difference is "real," the rearing methods affect intelligence (at odds of 19 to 1), the conclusion being that the two groups of rats must be samples from different populations. The point for our present purposes is that no such populations exist, apart from the "samples." No one has ever reared rats in these two ways or tested them, except in this experiment. This is the extreme case, but it applies whenever new procedures or new kinds of equipment are being compared. In less extreme cases a test of significance may seem to refer to existing populations, as for example in comparing verbal ability in sixth-grade boys and girls, but even here the procedure logically assumes an infinitely large population of verbal test scores, asks whether the two samples (boys' scores and girls') could have come from that one population, and does not restrict consideration to boys and girls now in the sixth grade or even to boys and girls who have ever lived.

In determining the error of measurement, a similiar assumption is made of sampling from an imaginary population. A chemist will tell you that the atomic weight of hydrogen as measured is 1.0079 plus or minus .0001. What he is saying is that there is a true value, but it cannot be known (the exact sciences have no exact answers; truth is elusive, *every* measurement has its probable error); there is a two-thirds probability that it lies between 1.0078 and 1.0080, or a 19-out-of-20 probability of being greater than 1.0077 and less than 1.0081, the most probable single estimate being 1.0079. I emphasize the detail to show how the physical scientist in his research for truth and avoidance of over-statement achieves his result by appeal to certain imaginary operations; for the probabilities referred to are obtained, logically, from the distribution of an infinitely large but nonexistent set of measurements with a mean of 1.0079 and a standard deviation of .0001.

LAW IN ANOTHER ASPECT

In this discussion I have tried to show that scientists, including the most hard-headed, deal freely and must deal with a universe that can be known only in thought, in some of its important features. If an electron or a photon is too small to be perceived, a continent is too large. The purpose is to put the problems of cause and effect and scientific law and order in a different light from what is usual. One might say, on the basis of the discussion of the preceding chapter, that determinism and such untestable propositions as the first law of motion are simply rules of thought, ways of looking at existence. But that falls short of reality in its implicit separation of the thinker from the object of thought, for what I have been trying to show is that what the scientist actually deals with is not separate from his thought. Determinism and law are not avenues of approach to the universe of the scientist but integral features of it. He can know and live in a universe, fragmentarily perceived, in which absolute order prevails even while he is fully aware of the vagaries that are features of ordinary experience and the vagaries of experimental data. Even more, he can inhabit two different universes at different times, deterministic when in his laboratory, indeterministic when he is trying to think philosophically about mind as an immaterial agent acting on a material brain. "Chance" and the impossibility of precise measurement can be features of a universe of absolute order, for it is also seen as one in which a human being can establish only limited control and can have at any moment only a limited amount of the information needed for prediction.

Obviously the scientist's world changes in detail with the advent of new knowledge, and sometimes is transformed in the course of what Kuhn has named scientific revolutions. It took a revolution to establish the first law of motion in place of Aristotelian ideas, but today it would take a bigger one to disestablish the law of the conservation of mass-energy. These examples of what I called true laws, because they cannot be falsified, can now be seen to have a higher validity than those that consist of empirical summations ("planets move in elliptical orbits," "a different atomic weight means a different chemical identity," "all swans are white"). This is because they are essential structural elements in the current universe of the physical scientist.

Also, in that universe they are absolute truth, a commodity not otherwise dealt with in scientific investigation. The true law is not *a priori* in the sense that mathematical truth is *a priori*, and it is clear why the logician must deny it that status; but it is clear also that scientific thought, or even the logic of science, is misrepresented when all propositions are divided in two classes, analytic and synthetic, the latter comprehending on the same footing the proposition that all crows are black and the proposition that all copper conducts electricity. The first law of motion and the statement that two and two make four have a different logical status, but their truth value in the current state of normal science is about equal. Scientific thought is not understood if one does not see that at present the laws of motion are not only unquestioned, they are unquestionable.

The layman also has his unquestionables, although there is not the same unanimity in the lay world about which ones they are. In this chapter it is the scientist that I have discussed, but it is the nature of human thought that we are really concerned with here. Science provides good examples, but the lay world of imagination, different as it may be in its content—incorporating any or all of indeterminism, superstition, a personal deity, psychic phenomena, the truth of sacred writings or a bigoted aversion thereto—seems to parallel the scientific one in all other ways. When one considers the great part played by faith in scientific research as well as in teaching, and the amount that a scientist must accept on the authority of others, it is not as simple as it has seemed to distinguish scientific from religious thought. The religious or the superstitious with spirits and angels about them, or demons and witchcraft, live and guide themselves with respect to a hidden order not available to the senses. They too construct for themselves a world of the imagination, partly from what they in fact perceive, partly from ideas provided by others in childhood, and partly from the creative activity of their own minds. Possession of the capacity for thought makes us a thought-dominated species.

There is still, of course, the constant necessity of coming to terms with the environment, a state of affairs that is summed up in that magnificent scene from Conrad's *Lord Jim,* in which Stein diagnoses Jim's trouble in three words: "He is romantic," and Marlowe asks spontaneously, "What's good for it?" Stein in effect says that the only cure is death, that we are all romantics by the nature of the case, as living men and women. But a real world still exists. "A man that is born falls into a dream like a man who falls into the sea. If he tries to climb out into the air as inexperienced men do, he drowns—*nicht wahr?*" We cannot live in one element or the other, only in both.

References

Alpers, A. *Dolphins, the myth and the mammal.* Boston: Houghton Mifflin, 1961.

Asher, E. J. The inadequacy of current intelligence tests for testing Kentucky Mountain children. *Journal of Genetic Psychology,* 1935, *46,* 480–486.

Barber, B. Resistance by scientists to scientific discovery. *Science,* 1961, *134,* 596–602.

Bartlett, J. E. A. A case of organized visual hallucinations in an old man with cataract, and their relation to the phenomena of the phantom limb. *Brain,* 1951, *74,* 363–373.

Bogen, J. E. The other side of the brain: II. An appositional mind. *Bulletin of the Los Angeles Neurological Societies,* 1969, *34,* 135–162.

Boring, E. G. A history of introspection. *Psychological Bulletin,* 1953, *50,* 169–189.

Brogden, W. J. Sensory preconditioning. *Journal of Experimental Psychology,* 1939, *25,* 323–332.

Chow, K. L., Riesen, A. H., & Newell, F. W. Degeneration of retinal ganglion cells in infant chimpanzees reared in darkness. *Journal of Comparative Neurology,* 1957, *107,* 27–42.

Conant, J. B. *Science and common sense.* New Haven: Yale University Press, 1951.

Condon, W. S., & Sander, L. W. Neonate movement is synchronized with adult speech: interactional participation and language acquisition. *Science,* 1974, *183,* 99–101.

Diaconis, P. Statistical problems in ESP research. *Science,* 1978, *201,* 131–136.

Douglas, R. M., & Goddard, G. V. Long-term potentiation of the perforant path-granule cell synapse in the rat hippocampus. *Brain Research,* 1975, *86,* 205–215.

Eccles, J. C. *The neurophysiological basis of mind.* Oxford: Clarendon Press, 1953.

Eccles, J. C. *The understanding of the brain.* New York: McGraw-Hill, 1973.

Fantz, R. L. The origin of form perception. *Scientific American,* May, 1961.

Feldman, M. W., & Lewontin, R. C. The heritability hang-up. *Science,* 1975, *190,* 1163–1168.

Forgays, D. G., & Forgays, J. W. The nature of the effect of free-environmental experience in the rat. *Journal of Comparative and Physiological Psychology,* 1952, *45,* 322–328.

Gazzaniga, M. S. *The bisected brain.* New York: Appleton-Century-Crofts, 1970.

Ghiselin, B. (Ed.). *The creative process.* New York: Mentor, 1955.

Gibson, J. J. A critical review of the concept of set in contemporary psychology. *Psychological Bulletin,* 1941, *38,* 781–817.

Gibson, J. J. *The perception of the visual world.* Boston: Houghton-Mifflin, 1950.

Goldfarb, W. Effects of early institutional care on adolescent personality. *Journal of Experimental Education,* 1943, *12,* 106–129.

Gordon, H. *Mental and scholastic tests among retarded children.* London: H.M. Stationery Office, 1928.

Goudge, T. A. *The thought of C. S. Peirce.* New York: Dover, 1969.

Hadamard, J. *The psychology of invention in the mathematical field.* New York: Dover, 1954.

Hansel, C. E. M. *ESP: a scientific evaluation.* New York: Scribner, 1966.

Hanson, N. R. *Patterns of discovery.* Cambridge (Eng.): Cambridge University Press, 1958.

Harlow, H. F. *Learning to love.* San Francisco: Albion, 1971.

Hayes, C. *The ape in our house.* New York: Harper, 1951.

Hayes, K. J., & Hayes, C. Imitation in a home-reared chimpanzee. *Journal of Comparative and Physiological Psychology,* 1952, *45,* 450–459.

Hebb, D. O. On the nature of fear. *Psychological Review,* 1946, *53,* 259–276.

Hebb, D. O. *The organization of behavior.* New York: Wiley, 1949.

Hebb, D. O. The American Revolution. *American Psychologist,* 1960, *15,* 735–745.

Hebb, D. O. The semiautonomous process, its nature and nurture. *American Psychologist,* 1963, *18,* 16–27.

Hebb, D. O. Concerning imagery. *Psychological Review,* 1968, *75,* 466–477.

Hebb, D. O. *Textbook of psychology* (3rd ed.). Philadelphia: Saunders, 1972.

Hebb, D. O. What psychology is about. *American Psychologist,* 1974, *29,* p. 77.

Hebb, D. O., Lambert, W. E., & Tucker, G. R. Language, thought and experience. *Modern Language Journal,* 1971, *55,* 212–222.

Hebb, D. O., & Thompson, W. R. The social significance of animal studies. In G. Lindzey (Ed.), *Handbook of Social Psychology.* Cambridge (Mass.): Addison-Wesley, 1968. Vol. 2.

Hebb, D. O., & Williams, K. A method of rating animal intelligence. *Journal of General Psychology,* 1946, *34,* 59–65.

Heron, W. The pathology of boredom. *Scientific American,* January, 1957.

Hilgard, E. R. *Divided consciousness: multiple controls in human thought and action.* New York: Wiley, 1977.

Hilgard, E. R., & Marquis, D. G. *Conditioning and learning.* New York: Appleton-Century, 1940.

Holloway, R. L. The casts of fossil hominid brains. *Scientific American,* 1974 (July), *231,* 106–115.

Hubel, D. H., & Wiesel, T. N. Receptive fields, binocular interaction and functional architecture in the cat's visual cortex. *Journal of Physiology,* 1962, *160,* 106–154.

Hubel, D. H., & Wiesel, T. N. Effects of visual deprivation on morphology and physiology of cells in the cat's lateral geniculate body. *Journal of Neurophysiology,* 1963, *26,* 978–993.

Humphrey, G. *Thinking.* London: Methuen, 1951.

Hunter, W. S. The delayed reaction in animals and children. *Behavior Monographs,* 1913, *2,* No. 6.

Huxley, J. Higher and lower organization in perception. *Journal of the Royal College of Physicians of Edinburgh,* 1962, *7,* 160–170.

Hymovitch, B. The effects of experiential variations on problem-solving in the rat. *Journal of Comparative and Physiological Psychology,* 1952, *45,* 313–321.

James, W. *Principles of psychology.* New York: Holt, 1890.

Jerison, H. J. *Evolution of the brain and intelligence.* New York: Academic Press, 1973.

Jones, H. E., & Jones, M. C. A study of fear. *Childhood Education,* 1928, *5,* 136–143.

Kellogg, W. N. *Porpoises and sonar.* Chicago: University of Chicago Press, 1961.

Kimura, D., & Archibald, Y. Motor functions of the right hemisphere. *Brain,* 1974, *97,* 337–350.

Köhler, W. *The mentality of apes.* New York: Harcourt, Brace, 1927.

Kuhn, T. S. *The structure of scientific revolutions.* Chicago: University of Chicago Press, 1962.

Lashley, K. S. Basic neural mechanisms in behavior. *Psychological Review,* 1930, *37,* 1–24.

Lashley, K. S. In search of the engram. *Symposia of the Society for Experimental Biology*, 1950, *4*, 454–482.

Levy, J., Trevarthen, C., & Sperry, R. W. Perception of bilateral chimeric figures following hemispheric deconnection. *Brain*, 1972, *95*, 61–78.

Lindbergh, C. *Saturday Evening Post*, 1953, June 6, p. 30.

Lindsley, D. B. Emotion. In S. S. Stevens (Ed.), *Handbook of Experimental Psychology*. New York: Wiley, 1951.

Loehlin, J. C., Lindzey, G., & Spuhler, J. N. *Race differences in intelligence*. San Francisco: Freeman, 1975.

McBride, A. F., & Hebb, D. O. Behavior of the captive bottle-nose dolphin, *Tursiops truncatus*. *Journal of Comparative and Physiological Psychology*, 1948, *41*, 111–123.

Melzack, R., & Scott, T. H. The effects of early experience on the response to pain. *Journal of Comparative and Physiological Psychology*, 1957, *50*, 155–161.

Milner, P. M. The cell assembly: Mark II. *Psychological Review*, 1957, *64*, 242–262.

Mountcastle, V. B. The view from within: pathways to the study of perception. *Johns Hopkins Medical Journal*, 1975, *136*, 109–131.

Murphy, G. *The challenge of psychical research*. New York: Harper, 1961.

Nissen, H. W., & Crawford, M. P. A preliminary study of food-sharing in young chimpanzees. *Journal of Comparative Psychology*, 1936, *22*, 393–419.

Ogden, R. M. Oswald Külpe and the Würzburg School. *American Journal of Psychology*, 1951, *64*, 4–19.

Parker, G. H. Proceedings of the American Philosophical Society, 1911, *50*, p. 224.

Popper, K. R. *Objective knowledge: an evolutionary approach*. Oxford: Clarendon Press, 1972.

Popper, K. R., & Eccles, J. C. *The self and its brain*. New York: Springer-Verlag, 1977.

Porter, P. B., Another puzzle picture. *American Journal of Psychology*, 1954, *67*, p. 550.

Pritchard, R. M. Stabilized images on the retina. *Scientific American*, 1961, *204* (June), 72–78.

Pritchard, R. M., Heron, W., & Hebb, D. O. Visual perception approached by the method of stabilized images. *Canadian Journal of Psychology*, 1960, *14*, 67–77.

Rabinovitch, M. S., & Rosvold, H. E. A closed-field intelligence test for rats. *Canadian Journal of Psychology*, 1951, *4*, 122–128.

Rakic, Pasko. Local circuit neurons. *Neurosciences Research Progress Bulletin*, 1975, *13*, no. 3.

Reichenbach, H. *The rise of scientific philosophy*. Berkeley: University of California Press, 1951.

Riesen, A. H. The development of visual perception in man and chimpanzee. *Science*, 1947, *106*, 107–108.

Russell, B. *History of Western Philosophy*. London: Allen & Unwin, 1961.

Ryle, G. *The concept of mind*. London: Hutchinson's University Library, 1949.

Scott, A. C. *Neurophysics*. New York: Wiley, 1977.

Siebenaler, J. B., & Caldwell, D. K. Cooperation among adult dolphins. *Journal of Mammalogy*, 1956, *37*, 126–128.

Siegel, R. K., & West, L. J. (Eds.). *Hallucinations: Behavior, experience and theory*. New York: Wiley, 1975.

Skinner, B. F. *Beyond freedom and dignity*. New York: Knopf, 1971.

Slobin, D. I. Comments on developmental psycholinguistics. In F. Smith & G. A. Miller (Eds.), *The genesis of language*. Cambridge (Mass.): M.I.T. Press, 1966.

Sperry, R. W. Hemispheric deconnection and unity in conscious awareness. *American Psychologist*, 1968, *23*, 723–733.

Sperry, R. W. Perception in the absence of the neocortical commissures. *Research Publications of the Association for Research in Nervous and Mental Disease*, 1970, *48* 123–138.

Thompson, W. R., & Heron, W. The effects of restricting experience on the problem-solving capacity of dogs. *Canadian Journal of Psychology*, 1954, *8*, 17–31.

Tinbergen, N. *The study of instinct*. Oxford: Clarendon Press, 1951.

Tinklepaugh, O. L. An experimental study of representative factors in monkeys. *Journal of Comparative Psychology,* 1928, *8,* 197–236.

Tyhurst, J. S. Individual reactions to community disaster: the natural history of psychiatric phenomena. *American Journal of Psychiatry, 1951, 107,* 764–769.

Vanderwolf, C. H. The role of the cerebral cortex and ascending activating systems in the control of behavior. In E. Satinoff & P. Teitelbaum (Eds.), *Handbook of Behavioral Neurobiology.* New York: Plenum, 1976.

von Bonin, G. *The evolution of the human brain.* Chicago: University of Chicago Press, 1963.

von Senden, M. *Raum-und Gestaltauffassung bei operierten Blindgeborenen vor und nach der Operation.* Leipzig: Barth, 1932.

von Senden, M. *Space and sight.* (Trans. P. Heath.) London: Methuen, 1960.

Weisenburg, T., Roe, A., & McBride, K.E. Adult intelligence: A psychological study of test performance. New York: Commonwealth Fund, 1936.

Wellman, B. L. Iowa studies on the effect of schooling. *Yearbook of the National Society for the Study of Education,* 1940, *39,* 377–399.

Wilson, E. O. Sociobiology: the new synthesis. Cambridge (Mass.): Belknap Press of Harvard University, 1975.

Woodworth, R. S. *Experimental psychology.* New York: Holt, 1938.

Yerkes, R. M. Psychological examining in the United States Army. *Memoirs of the National Academy of Science,* 1921, No. 15.

Author Index

Subject Index